STUDY WITH PURPOSE

# REVELATION: BIBLE STUDY GUIDE

## VOLUME 1

The Seven Churches

EDITORIAL KALH'EL

ISBN: 9781087891064

Imprint: LS Company

# Table of Contents

The Importance of Prophecy ........................................................................................................... 5

God's Character Revealed Through Jesus ................................................................................... 11

John the Revelator ......................................................................................................................... 17

The Book of Revelation ................................................................................................................. 23

Christ in the Heavenly Sanctuary ................................................................................................. 29

The Seven Churches ...................................................................................................................... 35

Ephesus ........................................................................................................................................... 41

Smyrna ............................................................................................................................................ 47

Pergamos ......................................................................................................................................... 53

Thyatira ........................................................................................................................................... 59

Sardis ............................................................................................................................................... 65

Philadelphia .................................................................................................................................... 71

Laodicea .......................................................................................................................................... 77

# The Importance of Prophecy

Lesson 1

*"Surely the Lord God will do nothing, but he revealeth his secret unto his servants the prophets"*

*(Amos 3:7)*

"As we near the close of this world's history, the prophecies relating to the last days especially demand our study."
*Christ's Object Lessons, p. 133.*

**Suggested Readings**: Prophets and Kings, pp. 722–733, The Acts of the Apostles, pp. 25–28.

**January 1**

1. **IN THE BEGINNING**

   a. **After creating man, how did God communicate with him? Genesis 1:28 (first part); 3:9. In what special sense can this kindle hope in our hearts?** Matthew 5:8.

The pure in heart live as in the visible presence of God during the time He apportions them in this world. And they will also see Him face to face in the future, immortal state, as did Adam when he walked and talked with God in Eden. 'Now we see through a glass, darkly; but then face to face' (1 Corinthians 13:12). –Thoughts From the Mount of Blessing, p. 27.

   b. **Describe the depth of the privilege extended to several of the early patriarchs.** Exodus 33:11.

It was the Son of God that gave to our first parents the promise of redemption. It was He who revealed Himself to the patriarchs. Adam, Noah, Abraham, Isaac, Jacob, and Moses understood the gospel. They looked for salvation through man's Substitute and Surety. These holy men of old held communion with the Saviour who was to come to our world in human flesh; and some of them talked with Christ and heavenly angels face to face. –Patriarchs and Prophets, p. 366.

January 2

## 2. DURING THE OLD DISPENSATION

    **a. What were the prophets called in old times, and why? 1 Samuel 9:9; Numbers 12:6; 24:16. Describe the important scene they beheld. Numbers 24:17.**

---

To Christ 'give all the prophets witness' (Acts 10:43). From the promise given to Adam, down through the patriarchal line and the legal economy, heaven's glorious light made plain the footsteps of the Redeemer. Seers beheld the Star of Bethlehem, the Shiloh to come, as future things swept before them in mysterious procession. In every sacrifice Christ's death was shown. In every cloud of incense His righteousness ascended. By every jubilee trumpet His name was sounded. In the awful mystery of the holy of holies His glory dwelt. –The Desire of Ages, pp. 211, 212.

    **b. What are some of the various deeds performed by God's prophets, and how are we all to benefit from their work? Hosea 12:13; Amos 3:7; 2 Chronicles 20:20.**

---

This is a time when every soul needs to cling earnestly to God. Those whom the Lord is leading to do His last work in the earth are to stand as Micah and Zephaniah and Zechariah stood in their day, to call to repentance and good works. The writings of these prophets contain warnings and instruction applicable to this time, and should receive our careful study. They should teach us to shun every phase of evil that made such warnings essential to the people of the past. Let every soul arouse and make diligent examination of self, that everything that would separate the people of God from righteousness may be put away. . . .

I would say to all our people, Place yourselves in the light, that you may reflect light, and that souls may be led to see the great and soul-saving truths of the Word of God. Every believer in Christ should be a laborer together with Him in drawing souls from sin to righteousness. We are to keep in view the life that measures with the life of God. We are to watch for opportunities to bring the truths of the Word before those who do not see and understand. Christ is not now with us in person, but through the agency of the Holy Spirit, He is present to impart His power and grace and great salvation." –The Review and Herald, September 16, 1909.

January 3

### 3. PROPHETS IN THE NEW TESTAMENT

    a. **What shows that the prophetic gift continued in New Testament times?** Acts 11:27, 28; 13:1; 21:8–11.

During the ages while the Scriptures of both the Old and the New Testament were being given, the Holy Spirit did not cease to communicate light to individual minds, apart from the revelations to be embodied in the Sacred Canon. The Bible itself relates how, through the Holy Spirit, men received warning, reproof, counsel, and instruction, in matters in no way relating to the giving of the Scriptures. And mention is made of prophets in different ages, of whose utterances nothing is recorded. In like manner, after the close of the canon of the Scriptures, the Holy Spirit was still to continue its work, to enlighten, warn, and comfort the children of God. –Lift Him Up, p. 118.

    b. **What characterizes the true church until the end of time?** Ephesians 4:11; 1 Corinthians 12:28. **What factors should awaken us to the importance of prophecy?**

'And the dragon was wroth with the woman, and went to make war with the remnant of her seed, which keep the commandments of God, and have the testimony of Jesus Christ' (Revelation 12:17). This prophecy points out clearly that the remnant church will acknowledge God in His law and will have the prophetic gift. Obedience to the law of God, and the spirit of prophecy has always distinguished the true people of God, and the test is usually given on present manifestations.

In Jeremiah's day the people had no question about the message of Moses, Elijah, or Elisha, but they did question and put aside the message sent of God to Jeremiah until its force and power was wasted and there was no remedy but for God to carry them away into captivity. . . .

As the third angel's message arose in the world, which is to reveal the law of God to the church in its fullness and power, the prophetic gift was also immediately restored. This gift has acted a very prominent part in the development and carrying forward of this message. –Loma Linda Messages, p. 33.

January 4

## 4. THE GIFT OF PROPHECY WITHDRAWN

**a. Why was the gift of the Holy Spirit, which includes the gift of prophecy, withdrawn from the Christian church for a time?** 1 Corinthians 13:8.

---

The Lord desires to make man the repository of divine influence, and the only thing that hinders the accomplishment of God's designs is that men close their hearts to the light of life. Apostasy caused the withdrawal of the Holy Spirit from man, but through the plan of redemption this blessing of heaven is to be restored to those who sincerely desire it. The Lord has promised to give all good things to those who ask Him, and all good things are defined as given with the gift of the Holy Spirit. –Manuscript Releases, vol. 2, p.11.

**b. What conditions can be expected when the gift of prophecy is either not present or not appreciated in the church?** Proverbs 29:18.

---

The Spirit of God is being withdrawn from the world, and those who have had great light and opportunities and have not improved them, will be the first to be left. They have grieved away the Spirit of God. The present activity of Satan in working upon hearts, and upon churches and nations should startle every student of prophecy. The end is near. –Selected Messages, bk. 3, p. 154.

[The] reasoning will be heard today from worldly-wise men, from the unfaithful watchmen in the pulpits, 'My Lord delayeth his coming, all things remain as they were from the beginning. You have no need to be alarmed, there is to be a thousand years of temporal millennium before Christ will come. All the world will be converted. Peace, peace; you should pay no regard to these fanatics, who are only alarmists.' The world generally will despise prophecy and abuse those who speak to them the words of God, rebuking their sins and calling them to repentance. –The Signs of the Times, January 3, 1878.

I know your danger. If you lose confidence in the testimonies you will drift away from Bible truth. I have been fearful that many would take a questioning, doubting position, and in my distress for your souls I would warn you. How many will heed the warning? –Testimonies, vol. 5, p. 98.

January 5

## 5. THE PROPHETIC GIFT RESTORED

a. Why should we earnestly heed the counsel given by the apostle Peter regarding prophecy? 2 Peter 1:19-21; 3:1-7.

---

The laws of nature cannot prevent the fulfillment of God's word. The law is never greater than the Lawgiver, nor are the things created greater than the Creator. As it was in the days of Noah, so shall it be in the days of the Son of man. As men are warned of impending judgment, thousands will say, it cannot be. They will despise the truth, make light of prophecy, and deride the teacher of righteousness. One will turn aside to his farm, another to his merchandise, and care for none of these things. –The Signs of the Times, February 24, 1887.

Already the judgments of God are abroad in the land, as seen in storms, in floods, in tempests, in earthquakes, in peril by land and by sea. The great I AM is speaking to those who make void His law. When God's wrath is poured out upon the earth, who will then be able to stand? –Testimonies, vol. 5, p. 136.

b. **In view of the nearness of the end of time, what are we admonished to do?** 1 Thessalonians 5:20; Revelation 22:7.

---

The perils of the last days are upon us, and in our work we are to warn the people of the danger they are in. Let not the solemn scenes which prophecy has revealed, be left untouched. If our people were half awake, if they realized the nearness of the events portrayed in the Revelation, a reformation would be wrought in our churches, and many more would believe the message. –Evangelism, p. 195.

January 6

**REVIEW AND THOUGHT QUESTIONS**

1. How can we be sure to retain the gift of prophecy?

2. What acts were performed by the Old Testament prophets?

3. How were prophets used in the early Christian church?

4. Why was the gift of prophecy withdrawn?

5. What deserves our special attention in these last days?

# God's Character Revealed Through Jesus

Lesson 2

"God, who at sundry times and in divers manners spake in time past unto the fathers by the prophets, hath in these last days spoken unto us by his Son."

(Hebrews 1:1, 2)

"Christ came to the world to reveal the character of
the Father, and to redeem the fallen race." *The
Review and Herald, January 7, 1890.*

*Suggested Readings*: Steps to Christ, pp. 85–91. That I May Know Him, pp. 288, 289.

January 7

1. **THE LAW OF GOD**

   a. **What is revealed about God's character as represented in His moral law?** Psalm 119:142; Romans 7:12.

---

Christ came to this world to live the law and represent the character of God, that the delusions which Satan had brought upon the world might be dispelled. –The Signs of the Times, February 24, 1898.

   b. **What was Jesus' attitude in regard to the Ten Commandments?** Isaiah 42:21; John 15:10; Psalm 40:8.

---

The claim that Christ by His death abolished His Father's law is without foundation. Had it been possible for the law to be changed or set aside, then Christ need not have died to save man from the penalty of sin.–The Great Controversy, p. 466.

Though Christ did away with their multitudinous exactions, He explicitly declared that not one jot or tittle of the law should ever fail. He had come to exalt the law, to magnify the law and make it honorable. –The Review and Herald, April 30, 1895.

January 8

## 2. GOD WITH US

    a. **Who was Christ before His incarnation and what was His position?** John 1:1–4; Philippians 2:6.

---

Christ is the pre-existent, self-existent Son of God.... In speaking of His pre-existence, Christ carries the mind back through dateless ages. He assures us that there never was a time when He was not in close fellowship with the eternal God....

Christ was God essentially, and in the highest sense. He was with God from all eternity, God over all, blessed forevermore. The Lord Jesus Christ, the divine Son of God, existed from eternity, a distinct person, yet one with the Father. He was the surpassing glory of heaven. He was the commander of the heavenly intelligences, and the adoring homage of the angels was received by Him as His right." –The Faith I Live By, p. 46.

There are light and glory in the truth that Christ was one with the Father before the foundation of the world was laid. This is the light shining in a dark place, making it resplendent with divine, original glory. –The Review and Herald, April 5, 1906.

    b. **What constituted a miraculous sign about the incarnation of Jesus?** Isaiah 7:14; Matthew 1:23; Luke 1:34, 35.

---

The more we think about Christ's becoming a babe here on earth, the more wonderful it appears. How can it be that the helpless babe in Bethlehem's manger is still the divine Son of God? Though we cannot understand it, we can believe that He who made the worlds, for our sakes became a helpless babe. Though higher than any of the angels, though as great as the Father on the throne of heaven, He became one with us. In Him God and man became one, and it is in this fact that we find the hope of our fallen race. Looking upon Christ in the flesh, we look upon God in humanity, and see in Him the brightness of divine glory, the express image of God the Father. –Selected Messages, bk. 3, pp. 127, 128.

[Jesus Christ] was 'the image of God,' the image of His greatness and majesty, 'the outshining of His glory.' It was to manifest this glory that He came to our world. To this sin-darkened earth He came to reveal the light of God's love–to be 'God with us.' Therefore it was prophesied of Him, 'His name shall be called Immanuel.' –The Desire of Ages, p. 19.

January 9

## 3. SPEAKING THROUGH PROPHETS AND APOSTLES

   a. **Who spoke to Moses on Mount Sinai and gave him the Ten Commandments written on two tables of stone?** Acts 7:38; 1 Corinthians 10:4.

---

It was Christ who spoke the law from Sinai. It was Christ who gave the law to Moses, engraven on tables of stone. –The Review and Herald, September 27, 1881.

Christ was not only the leader of the Hebrews in the wilderness–the Angel in whom was the name of Jehovah, and who, veiled in the cloudy pillar, went before the host–but it was He who gave the law to Israel. Amid the awful glory of Sinai, Christ declared in the hearing of all the people the ten precepts of His Father's law. . . . It was Christ that spoke to His people through the prophets. –Patriarchs and Prophets, p. 366.

Through patriarchs and prophets [Christ] revealed His truth to His people. Christ was the teacher of His ancient people as verily as He was when He came to the world clothed in the garments of humanity. Hiding His glory in human form, He often appeared to His people and talked with them 'face to face, as a man speaketh unto his friend.' He, their invisible Leader, was enshrouded in the pillar of fire and of cloud, and spoke to His people through Moses. –Lift Him Up, p. 314.

   b. **When Jesus was on earth, what did He affirm about His real identity?** John 8:58; 13:13.

---

The teaching of Christ in the gospel is in perfect harmony with the teaching of Christ through the prophets in the Old Testament. The prophets spoke through the messengers of Christ in the Old Testament as much as the apostles voiced His messages in the New Testament, and there is no contradiction between their teachings. –Selected Messages, 1, p. 345.

It was by His word that Jesus healed disease and cast out demons; by His word He stilled the sea, and raised the dead; and the people bore witness that His word was with power. He spoke the word of God, as He had spoken through all the prophets and teachers of the Old Testament. The whole Bible is a manifestation of Christ, and the Saviour desired to fix the faith of His followers on the word. –The Desire of Ages, p. 390.

January 10

## 4. CALLED TO BE WITNESSES

    a. **Just before His ascension, what did Jesus request from the disciples? Luke 24:49; Acts 1:4. What must we realize about the Holy Spirit?**

---

A determined, vigilant leader was in command of the agencies of evil, and the followers of Christ could resist and overcome the powers of darkness only through the help that God could give them. But through the power of the Holy Spirit [the disciples] were to be successful witnesses of Christ to the uttermost parts of the earth. Beginning at Jerusalem, they were to widen the scene of their operations until all nations should hear the sound of the gospel. –The Review and Herald, November 6, 1894.

Christ has promised the gift of the Holy Spirit to His church, and the promise belongs to us as much as to the first disciples. But like every other promise, it is given on conditions. There are many who believe and profess to claim the Lord's promise; they talk about Christ and about the Holy Spirit, yet receive no benefit. They do not surrender the soul to be guided and controlled by the divine agencies. We cannot use the Holy Spirit. The Spirit is to use us. –The Desire of Ages, p. 672. [Author's italics.]

    b. **What is involved in the gospel commission and how far does it extend? Matthew 28:18–20; Acts 1:8.**

---

The Saviour's commission to the disciples included all the believers. It includes all believers in Christ to the end of time. It is a fatal mistake to suppose that the work of saving souls depends alone on the ordained minister. . . . All who receive the life of Christ are ordained to work for the salvation of their fellow men. For this work the church was established, and all who take upon themselves its sacred vows are thereby pledged to be coworkers with Christ. –The Desire of Ages, p. 822.

Christ urges again and again upon His disciples the obligation to make known the gospel to the world. When within one step of the throne of God, He opened their understanding, that they might know the Scriptures, repeating again the old commandment to go forth and preach the message of salvation. –The Review and Herald, November 6, 1894.

January 11

## 5. THE POWER OF THE HOLY SPIRIT

    a. **According to the promise of Jesus, what event took place ten days after His ascension and what was the result?** Acts 2:1–4, 16–18, 41.

That the disciples of Christ might be prepared for the great work which they were to do, Jesus had instructed them to tarry in Jerusalem until they should be endowed with power from on high. On the day of Pentecost, as they were assembled together, and with one accord were seeking for the fulfillment of His promise, the Spirit of God descended, and the hearts of those who believed were filled with the Holy Ghost. The most signal evidence of the power of God was manifested, and thousands were converted in a day. –The Signs of the Times, June 9, 1890.

    b. **In these last days of earth's history, what promise is given us and what will be its result?** Joel 2:28, 29; Acts 3:19.

As the 'former rain' was given, in the outpouring of the Holy Spirit at the opening of the gospel, to cause the upspringing of the precious seed, so the 'latter rain' will be given at its close for the ripening of the harvest.... The great work of the gospel is not to close with less manifestation of the power of God than marked its opening. The prophecies which were fulfilled in the outpouring of the former rain at the opening of the gospel are again to be fulfilled in the latter rain at its close. –The Great Controversy, pp. 611, 612.

January 12

**REVIEW AND THOUGHT QUESTIONS**

1. What relationship exists between Christ and the law?

_____

_____

2. What miracle can we not now fully understand?

_____

_____

3. How does Christ communicate with His people?

_____

_____

4. What is our great duty as Christians?

_____

_____

5. What will help us in the fulfillment of our commission?

_____

_____

# John the Revelator

Lesson 3

"I John, who also am your brother, and companion in tribulation, and in the kingdom and patience of Jesus Christ."

(Revelation 1:9)

To John the Lord Jesus opened the subjects that He
saw would be needed by His people in the last days.
–*The Review and Herald*, October 22, 1903.

***Suggested Readings***: The Sanctified Life, pp. 69–79. The Acts of the Apostles, pp. 568–577.

January 14

## 1. THE BELOVED DISCIPLE

a. **Which of the disciples were the closest with Jesus?** Mark 5:37; Matthew 17:1. **Of these three who was still closer, and why?**

John and James, Andrew and Peter, with Philip, Nathanael, and Matthew, had been more closely connected with Him than the others, and had witnessed more of His miracles. Peter, James, and John stood in still nearer relationship to Him. They were almost constantly with Him, witnessing His miracles, and hearing His words. John pressed into still closer intimacy with Jesus, so that he is distinguished as the one whom Jesus loved. The Saviour loved them all, but John's was the most receptive spirit. He was younger than the others, and with more of the child's confiding trust he opened his heart to Jesus. –The Desire of Ages, p. 292.

b. **What was the main subject that attracted the attention of John?** John 13:34, 35; 1 John 3:11.

The apostle John realized that brotherly love was waning in the church, and he dwelt particularly upon this point. Up to the day of his death he urged upon believers the constant exercise of love for one another.–Testimonies, vol. 8, p. 241.

January 15

## 2. TRANSFORMED BY GRACE

   a. **What was the character of John like in his early experience in the gospel ministry?** Mark 3:17; Luke 9:51–56.

---

John and his brother were called the 'sons of thunder.' John was a man of decided character, but he had learned lessons from the great Teacher. He had defects of character, and any slight shown to Jesus aroused his indignation and combativeness. His love for Christ was the love of a soul saved through the merits of Jesus; but with this love there were natural evil traits that had to be overcome. At one time he and his brother claimed the right to the highest position in the kingdom of heaven, and at another he forbade a man to cast out devils and heal diseases because he followed not with the disciples. At another time when he saw his Lord slighted by the Samaritans he wanted to call down fire from heaven to consume them. But Christ rebuked him, saying, 'The Son of man is not come to destroy men's lives, but to save them.' –The Signs of the Times, April 20, 1891.

   b. **By what means was John, "the son of thunder," transformed into an apostle of love?** Hebrews 12:1, 2.

---

John was a living illustration of sanctification. On the other hand, Judas possessed a form of godliness, while his character was more satanic than divine. He professed to be a disciple of Christ, but in words and in works denied Him.

Judas had the same precious opportunities as had John to study and to imitate the Pattern. He listened to the lessons of Christ, and his character might have been transformed by divine grace. But while John was earnestly warring against his own faults and seeking to assimilate to Christ, Judas was violating his conscience, yielding to temptation, and fastening upon himself habits of dishonesty that would transform him into the image of Satan. –The Sanctified Life, pp. 59, 60.

It is the Holy Spirit, the Comforter, which Jesus said He would send into the world, that changes our character into the image of Christ; and when this is accomplished, we reflect, as in a mirror, the glory of the Lord. That is, the character of the one who thus beholds Christ is so like His, that one looking at him sees Christ's own character shining out. –Our High Calling, p. 58.

January 16

## 3. PERSECUTION OF THE CHRISTIANS

a. **What prediction of Jesus was fulfilled in the lives of the early Christians?** John 15:20; 16:2.

---

One after another the foremost of the builders fell by the hand of the enemy. Stephen was stoned; James was slain by the sword; Paul was beheaded; Peter was crucified; John was exiled. Yet the church grew. New workers took the place of those who fell, and stone after stone was added to the building. Thus slowly ascended the temple of the church of God.

Centuries of fierce persecution followed the establishment of the Christian church, but there were never wanting men who counted the work of building God's temple dearer than life itself. Of such it is written: "Others had trial of cruel mockings and scourgings, yea, moreover of bonds and imprisonment: they were stoned, they were sawn asunder, were tempted, were slain with the sword: they wandered about in sheepskins and goatskins; being destitute, afflicted, tormented; (of whom the world was not worthy:) they wandered in deserts, and in mountains, and in dens and caves of the earth' (Hebrews 11:36–38)." –The Acts of the Apostles, pp. 597, 598.

b. **What happened to John in the time of persecution, and what promise was then fulfilled?** Isaiah 43:2; Job 23:10.

---

John was cast into a caldron of boiling oil; but the Lord preserved the life of His faithful servant, even as He preserved the three Hebrews in the fiery furnace. As the words were spoken, Thus perish all who believe in that deceiver, Jesus Christ of Nazareth, John declared, My Master patiently submitted to all that Satan and his angels could devise to humiliate and torture Him. He gave His life to save the world. I am honored in being permitted to suffer for His sake. I am a weak, sinful man. Christ was holy, harmless, undefiled. He did no sin, neither was guile found in His mouth. These words had their influence, and John was removed from the caldron by the very men who had cast him in.

Again the hand of persecution fell heavily upon the apostle. By the emperor's decree John was banished to the Isle of Patmos, condemned 'for the word of God, and for the testimony of Jesus Christ' (Revelation 1:9). –The Acts of the Apostles, p. 570.

January 17

## 4. ON THE ISLE OF PATMOS

a. **In order to silence the voice of John, what did the enemies of the gospel do to him after he had been saved from the boiling oil?** Revelation 1:9.

---

Again the enemies of truth sought to silence the voice of the faithful witness. John was banished to the Isle of Patmos. Here, they thought, he could no longer trouble Israel, and he must finally die of hardship and distress. –The Signs of the Times, March 22, 1905.

John, the beloved disciple, was exiled to lonely Patmos, that he might be separated from all strife, and even from the work he loved, and that the Lord might commune with him and open before him the closing scenes in this earth's history. –The Review and Herald, June 14, 1887.

Patmos, a barren, rocky island in the Aegean Sea, had been chosen by the Roman government as a place of banishment for criminals; but to the servant of God this gloomy abode became the gate of heaven. Here, shut away from the busy scenes of life, and from the active labors of former years, he had the companionship of God and Christ and the heavenly angels, and from them he received instruction for the church for all future time. The events that would take place in the closing scenes of this earth's history were outlined before him; and there he wrote out the visions he received from God. –The Acts of the Apostles, pp. 570, 571.

b. **How did John improve the opportunities granted to him while on Patmos?** 2 Timothy 4:2.

---

The history of John affords a striking illustration of the way in which God can use aged workers. When John was exiled to the Isle of Patmos, there were many who thought him to be past service, an old and broken reed, ready to fall at any time. But the Lord saw fit to use him still. Though banished from the scenes of his former labor, he did not cease to bear witness to the truth. Even in Patmos he made friends and converts. His was a message of joy, proclaiming a risen Saviour who on high was interceding for His people until He should return to take them to Himself. –The Acts of the Apostles, pp. 572, 573.

January 18

## 5. THE LORD'S DAY

a. **What account does John give us of his first vision on the Isle of Patmos?** Revelation 1:10.

"I was in the Spirit on the Lord's day." Did John here mean Sunday?–There is but one day called the Lord's day, and that is the seventh day of the week, the Sabbath instituted at creation. –The Signs of the Times, May 13, 1897.

It was on the Sabbath that the Lord of glory appeared to the exiled apostle. The Sabbath was as sacredly observed by John on Patmos as when he was preaching to the people in the towns and cities of Judea. He claimed as his own the precious promises that had been given regarding that day. –The Acts of the Apostles, p. 581.

b. **What promise is given to those who respect and honor the Sabbath?** Isaiah 56:6, 7; 58:13, 14.

John remembered that one of these ten precepts called upon him to 'remember the Sabbath day to keep it holy.' And the Lord's day, the day on which Jehovah rested after the great work of creation, and which He blessed and sanctified, was as sacredly observed by him upon the lonely isle as it had been when he was among the churches, worshiping with them on that holy day.–The Signs of the Times, February 5, 1885.

To all who receive the Sabbath as a sign of Christ's creative and redeeming power, it will be a delight.–The Desire of Ages, p. 289.

January 19

**REVIEW AND THOUGHT QUESTIONS**

1. How did John become the beloved disciple?

2. How can we have the transformation experienced by John?

3. What will happen to all who follow Christ?

4. Even in adversity, what is always the Christian's duty?

5. What reveals the magnitude of John's Sabbathkeeping?

# The Book of Revelation

Lesson 4

"Behold, I come quickly: blessed is he that keepeth the sayings of the prophecy of this book."

(Revelation 22:7)

"In the Revelation all the books of the Bible meet
and end. Here is the complement of the book of
Daniel. One is a prophecy; the other a revelation."
*The Acts of the Apostles, p. 585.*

**Suggested Readings**: The Acts of the Apostles, pp. 578–585. Early Writings, pp. 110, 285–289.

January 21

## 1. REVELATION – NOT A MYSTERY

a. Who is the author of the book of Revelation? Revelation 1:1. What is the meaning of the word "Revelation"?

God gave [the] revelation [of the truth for these last days] to Christ, and Christ communicated the same to John. –The SDA Bible Commentary [E. G. White Comments], vol. 7, p. 953.

In the past teachers have declared Daniel and the Revelation to be sealed books, and the people have turned from them. The veil whose apparent mystery has kept many from lifting it, God's own hand has withdrawn from these portions of His word. The very name 'Revelation' contradicts the statement that it is a sealed book. 'Revelation' means that something of importance is revealed. The truths of this book are addressed to those living in these last days. –Testimonies to Ministers, p. 113.

b. Why is it that many do not appreciate the study of the book of Revelation? 2 Timothy 4:3, 4; 2 Corinthians 4:3.

The study of the Revelation directs the mind to the prophecies of Daniel, and both present most important instruction, given of God to men, concerning events to take place at the close of this world's history. –The Great Controversy, p. 341.

January 22

## 2. WRITTEN FOR THE CHRISTIAN DISPENSATION

    **a. What can we understand from the words "which must shortly come to pass" written in Revelation 1:1?**

---

Christ came to John exiled on the Isle of Patmos to give him the truth for these last days, to show him that which must shortly come to pass. Jesus Christ is the great trustee of divine revelation. It is through Him that we have a knowledge of what we are to look for in the closing scenes of this earth's history. –The SDA Bible Commentary [E. G. White Comments], vol. 7, p. 953.

The book of Revelation, in connection with the book of Daniel, especially demands study. Let every God-fearing teacher consider how most clearly to comprehend and to present the gospel that our Saviour came in person to make known to His servant John–'The Revelation of Jesus Christ, which God gave unto Him, to show unto His servants things which must shortly come to pass' (Revelation 1:1)....

"Blessed is he that readeth, and they that hear the words of this prophecy, and keep those things which are written therein: for the time is at hand" (Revelation 1:3)." –Education, p. 191.

    **b. Why is it important to heed the messages contained in the book of Revelation?** Revelation 1:3.

---

It was Gabriel, 'His angel,' whom Christ sent to open the future to the beloved John; and a blessing is pronounced on those who read and hear the words of the prophecy, and keep the things written therein. . . . God has given these things to us, and His blessing will attend the reverent, prayerful study of the prophetic scriptures. –The Desire of Ages, p. 234.

The Lord will bless all who will seek humbly and meekly to understand that which is revealed in the Revelation. This book contains so much that is large with immortality and full of glory that all who read and search it earnestly receive the blessing to those 'that hear the words of this prophecy, and keep those things which are written therein.' One thing will certainly be understood from the study of Revelation–that the connection between God and His people is close and decided. –The Faith I Live By, p. 345.

January 23

## 3. A WONDERFUL PROMISE

a. **What is the significance of the words used by John in his greetings to the churches in Asia?** Revelation 1:4–6.

---

Why is it that there are so many who feel in uncertainty, who feel that they are orphans?–It is because they do not cultivate faith in the precious assurance that the Lord Jesus is their sin-bearer.... We should daily exercise faith; and that faith should daily increase as it is exercised, as we realize that He has not only redeemed us, but has loved us, and washed us from our sins in His own blood, and has made us kings and priests unto God and the Father. –Sons and Daughters of God, p. 287.

The Lord would save us from the corruptions of the world; for He chose us in Christ before the foundation of the world, that we should be holy and without blame before Him in love. Jesus, our precious Saviour, has redeemed us and washed us from our sins in His own blood, and has clothed us with the garments of salvation, even in His own robe of righteousness. –The Signs of the Times, May 2, 1892.

b. **In the upper room, what assurance had the Saviour given to His disciples?** John 14:1–3. **When and how was this promise repeated and further described?** Acts 1:9–11.

---

It was the compassionate Saviour, who, anticipating the loneliness and sorrow of His followers, commissioned angels to comfort them with the assurance that He would come again in person, even as He went into heaven. –The Great Controversy, p. 339.

Jesus is coming, but not as at His first advent, a babe in Bethlehem; not as He rode into Jerusalem, when the disciples praised God with a loud voice and cried, 'Hosanna'; but in the glory of the Father and with all the retinue of holy angels to escort Him on His way to earth. All heaven will be emptied of the angels, while the waiting saints will be looking for Him and gazing into heaven, as were the men of Galilee when He ascended from the Mount of Olivet. Then only those who are holy, those who have followed fully the meek Pattern, will with rapturous joy exclaim as they behold Him, "Lo, this is our God; we have waited for Him, and He will save us."–Early Writings, p. 110.

January 24

## 4. A SOLEMN AND GLORIOUS PROMISE

a. **What prophetic event is repeated in the very first chapter of Revelation?** Revelation 1:7.

---

Many think lightly of Christ now. They despise and reject Him, and say, 'Where is the promise of his coming? for since the fathers fell asleep, all things continue as they were from the beginning.' But we read, 'He cometh with clouds; and every eye shall see him' (Revelation 1:7). The same Jesus whose atonement has been rejected, whose followers have been despised and reviled, will be revealed from heaven. –The Review and Herald, November 22, 1898.

b. **What else should we understand about this wondrous scene?** 1 Thessalonians 4:16–18; 2 Thessalonians 1:7–10.

---

One of the most solemn and yet most glorious truths revealed in the Bible is that of Christ's second coming to complete the great work of redemption. To God's pilgrim people, so long left to sojourn in 'the region and shadow of death,' a precious, joy-inspiring hope is given in the promise of His appearing, who is 'the resurrection and the life,' to 'bring home again His banished.' The doctrine of the second advent is the very keynote of the Sacred Scriptures. From the day when the first pair turned their sorrowing steps from Eden, the children of faith have waited the coming of the Promised One to break the destroyer's power and bring them again to the lost Paradise. Holy men of old looked forward to the advent of the Messiah in glory, as the consummation of their hope. –The Great Controversy, p. 299.

c. **As believers in Christ's glorious return, what solemn truths must we realize?** 1 John 3:2, 3; Matthew 16:27.

---

It is through faith in Jesus Christ that the truth is accepted in the heart, and the human agent is purified and cleansed. . . . He has an abiding principle in the soul, that enables him to overcome temptation. 'Whosoever abideth in him sinneth not.' God has power to keep the soul that is in Christ who is under temptation. –The SDA Bible Commentary [E. G. White Comments], vol. 7, p. 951.

January 25

## 5. AN APPROPRIATE TITLE

    a. **How does Jesus identify Himself to John the Revelator, and what truths does this signify?** Revelation 1:8.

When the students of prophecy shall set their hearts to know the truths of Revelation, they will realize what an importance is attached to this search. Christ Jesus is the Alpha and the Omega, the Genesis of the Old Testament, and the Revelation of the New. Both meet together in Christ. –The SDA Bible Commentary [E. G. White Comments], vol. 6, p. 1092.

The first gleam of light that pierced the gloom in which sin had wrapped the world, came from Christ. And from Him has come every ray of heaven's brightness that has fallen upon the inhabitants of the earth. In the plan of redemption Christ is the Alpha and the Omega–the First and the Last. –Patriarchs and Prophets, p. 367.

    b. **What distinct aspects of Jesus Christ should we keep in mind?** Revelation 22:12, 13.

What a Saviour we have! . . . None but just such an ever-living, mighty God, could pay the ransom to save sinners. –The Review and Herald, February 18, 1896.

The return of Christ to our world will not be long delayed. Let this be the keynote of every message.

The blessed hope of the second appearing of Christ, with its solemn realities, needs to be often presented to the people. Looking for the soon appearing of our Lord will lead us to regard earthly things as emptiness and nothingness." –Testimonies, vol. 6, p. 406.

January 26

**REVIEW AND THOUGHT QUESTIONS**

1. Why is the book of Revelation important in our days?

___

2. How should the Christian approach Revelation?

___

3. Why are many wandering in hopelessness?

___

4. What are some key aspects to Christ's second coming?

___

5. What is significant about the title "Alpha and Omega"?

___

# Christ in the Heavenly Sanctuary

Lesson 5

We have such an high priest . . . a minister of the sanctuary, and of the true tabernacle, which the Lord pitched, and not man.

(Hebrews 8:1-2)

The holy places of the sanctuary in heaven are represented by the two apartments in the sanctuary on earth. –The Great Controversy, p. 414.

**Suggested Readings**: The Great Controversy, pp. 409–422. Early Writings, pp. 250–253.

January 28

## 1. A REPLICA OF THE HEAVENLY

a. **When Moses spent forty days with the Lord on Mount Sinai, what specific instructions did he receive?** Exodus 25:8, 9, 40.

The sanctuary in heaven, in which Jesus ministers in our behalf, is the great original, of which the sanctuary built by Moses was a copy. God placed His Spirit upon the builders of the earthly sanctuary.–The Great Controversy, p. 414.

b. **With what was the earthly tabernacle constructed?** Exodus 25:1-7. **How was it divided?**

For the building of the sanctuary, great and extensive preparations were necessary; a large amount of the most precious and costly material was required, but the Lord accepted only freewill offerings.–Prophets and Kings, p. 61.

The tabernacle itself consisted of two apartments called the holy and the most holy place, separated by a rich and beautiful curtain, or veil.–The Great Controversy, p. 412.

January 29

## 2. THE MINISTRY IN THE HOLY PLACE

a. **What provision was made for those who ignorantly transgressed God's law?** Leviticus 4:27–31; Acts 17:30.

---

The most important part of the daily ministration was the service performed in behalf of individuals. The repentant sinner brought his offering to the door of the tabernacle, and placing his hand upon the victim's head, confessed his sins, thus in figure transferring them from himself to the innocent sacrifice. By his own hand the animal was then slain, and the blood was carried by the priest into the holy place and sprinkled before the veil, behind which was the ark containing the law that the sinner had transgressed. By this ceremony the sin was, through the blood, transferred in figure to the sanctuary. –The Faith I Live By, p. 198.

Such was the work that went on, day by day, throughout the year. The sins of Israel were thus transferred to the sanctuary, and a special work became necessary for their removal. –The Great Controversy, p. 418.

b. **What was the daily duty of the common priest in the first apartment of the earthly sanctuary?** Hebrews 9:6, 9, 10.

---

The daily service consisted of the morning and evening burnt offering, the offering of sweet incense on the golden altar, and the special offerings for individual sins. . . .

Every morning and evening a lamb of a year old was burned upon the altar, with its appropriate meat offering, thus symbolizing the daily consecration of the nation to Jehovah, and their constant dependence upon the atoning blood of Christ. God expressly directed that every offering presented for the service of the sanctuary should be 'without blemish' (Exodus 12:5). The priests were to examine all animals brought as a sacrifice, and were to reject every one in which a defect was discovered. Only an offering 'without blemish' could be a symbol of His perfect purity who was to offer Himself as 'a lamb without blemish and without spot' (1 Peter 1:19)." –Patriarchs and Prophets, p. 352.

January 30

## 3. THE WORK OF THE HIGH PRIEST

    a. **How was the high priest attired? Exodus 29:4–7. What was the difference between the garments of the common priests and those of the high priest?**

---

In accordance with their office, a special dress was appointed for the priests. 'Thou shalt make holy garments for Aaron thy brother, for glory and for beauty,' was the divine direction to Moses. The robe of the common priest was of white linen, and woven in one piece. It extended nearly to the feet and was confined about the waist by a white linen girdle embroidered in blue, purple, and red. A linen turban, or miter, completed his outer costume. . . .

The garments of the high priest were of costly material and beautiful workmanship, befitting his exalted station. In addition to the linen dress of the common priest, he wore a robe of blue, also woven in one piece. Around the skirt it was ornamented with golden bells, and pomegranates of blue, purple, and scarlet. Outside of this was the ephod, a shorter garment of gold, blue, purple, scarlet, and white. It was confined by a girdle of the same colors, beautifully wrought. The ephod was sleeveless, and on its gold-embroidered shoulder pieces were set two onyx stones, bearing the names of the twelve tribes of Israel." –Patriarchs and Prophets, pp. 350, 351.

    b. **What event took place on the tenth day of the seventh month in Israel? Leviticus 23:27–32. What solemn ceremony was performed by the high priest? Hebrews 9:3, 7.**

---

Once a year, on the great Day of Atonement, the priest entered the most holy place for the cleansing of the sanctuary. The work there performed completed the yearly round of ministration.–The Great Controversy, p. 419.

No mortal eye but that of the high priest was to look upon the inner apartment of the sanctuary. Only once a year could the priest enter there, and that after the most careful and solemn preparation. With trembling he went in before God, and the people in reverent silence awaited his return, their hearts uplifted in earnest prayer for the divine blessing.–Patriarchs and Prophets, p. 352.

January 31

## 4. THE REVELATOR'S FIRST VISION

a. **How is Christ described in John's first vision, and what was John's reaction upon seeing his Lord? What words of encouragement were given to him?** Revelation 1:14–19.

---

John, who has so loved his Lord, and who has steadfastly adhered to the truth in the face of imprisonment, stripes, and threatened death, cannot endure the excellent glory of Christ's presence, and falls to the earth as one stricken dead. Jesus then lays His hand upon the prostrate form of His servant, saying, 'Fear not; . . . I am he that liveth, and was dead; and, behold, I am alive for evermore' (Revelation 1:17, 18). John was strengthened to live in the presence of his glorified Lord, and then were presented before him in holy vision the purposes of God for future ages. The glorious attractions of the heavenly home were made known to him. He was permitted to look upon the throne of God. –The Sanctified Life, p. 78.

b. **What do the furniture and garments of Christ reveal about His ministry in this first vision?** Revelation 1:10, 12, 13. **Describe the scene which sister White was also shown.**

---

I was then bidden to take notice of the two apartments of the heavenly sanctuary. The curtain, or door, was opened, and I was permitted to enter. In the first apartment I saw the candlestick with seven lamps, the table of shewbread, the altar of incense, and the censer. –Early Writings, pp. 251, 252.

The ministration of the priest throughout the year in the first apartment of the sanctuary, 'within the veil' which formed the door and separated the holy place from the outer court, represents the work of ministration upon which Christ entered at His ascension. It was the work of the priest in the daily ministration to present before God the blood of the sin offering, also the incense which ascended with the prayers of Israel. So did Christ plead His blood before the Father in behalf of sinners, and present before Him also, with the precious fragrance of His own righteousness, the prayers of penitent believers. Such was the work of ministration in the first apartment of the sanctuary in heaven.–The Great Controversy, pp. 420, 421.

February 1

## 5. TWO PHASES OF MEDIATORIAL WORK

a. **What work was Jesus to perform in the heavenly sanctuary since His ascension?** Hebrews 8:3–6.

---

For eighteen centuries this work of ministration continued in the first apartment of the sanctuary. The blood of Christ, pleaded in behalf of penitent believers, secured their pardon and acceptance with the Father, yet their sins still remained upon the books of record. –The Great Controversy, p. 421.

b. **What work did Jesus undertake in 1844?** Daniel 8:14; Hebrews 9:11–15. **Why should we be aware of this final mediation?**

---

As in the typical service there was a work of atonement at the close of the year, so before Christ's work for the redemption of men is completed there is a work of atonement for the removal of sin from the sanctuary. This is the service which began when the 2300 days ended. . . .

As anciently the sins of the people were by faith placed upon the sin offering and through its blood transferred, in figure, to the earthly sanctuary, so in the new covenant the sins of the repentant are by faith placed upon Christ and transferred, in fact, to the heavenly sanctuary. And as the typical cleansing of the earthly was accomplished by the removal of the sins by which it had been polluted, so the actual cleansing of the heavenly is to be accomplished by the removal, or blotting out, of the sins which are there recorded." –The Great Controversy, pp. 421, 422.

February 2

**REVIEW AND THOUGHT QUESTIONS**

1. What gifts are acceptable to God?

2. What was the daily service performed in the sanctuary?

3. Why was the yearly work of the high priest so solemn?

4. What do we learn about Christ from John's first vision?

5. What began in the sanctuary in 1844?

# The Seven Churches

Lesson 6

"What thou seest, write in a book, and send it unto the seven churches which are in Asia."

(Revelation 1:11)

The Revelation was written to the seven churches in Asia, which represented the people of God throughout the world. –*The Signs of the Times, January 28, 1903.*

***Suggested Readings***: The Acts of the Apostles, pp. 585–592. God's Amazing Grace, p. 95.

February 4

## 1. THE STARS OF THE CHURCHES

a. **What do the stars that John saw in the hands of Jesus represent? Revelation 1:16, 20. Who are to preach the messages to the seven churches?**

God's ministers are symbolized by the seven stars, which He who is the first and the last has under His special care and protection. The sweet influences that are to be abundant in the church are bound up with these ministers of God, who are to represent the love of Christ. . . . They are but instruments in His hands, and all the good they accomplish is done through His power. –Gospel Workers, pp. 13, 14.

b. **What counsel is given to ministers so that they may faithfully fulfill their duties? 1 Corinthians 4:1, 2; 2 Corinthians 6:3–7. What are the results of unfaithful ministry?**

The people will seldom rise higher than their minister. A world-loving spirit in him has a tremendous influence upon others. The people make his deficiencies an excuse to cover their world-loving spirit. –Testimonies, vol. 2, pp. 645, 646.

February 5

## 2. THE SEVEN CANDLESTICKS

**a. What is the meaning of Jesus walking among the candlesticks found in Revelation 1:20?**

'These things saith He that holdeth the seven stars in His right hand, who walketh in the midst of the seven golden candlesticks, I know thy works.' This figure illustrates the eternal vigilance of our Saviour. Christ is in the midst of the seven golden candlesticks, walking from church to church, from congregation to congregation, from heart to heart. He who keeps Israel neither slumbers nor sleeps. If the candlesticks were left to the care of human beings, how often they would flicker and go out. But God has not given His church into the hands of men. Christ, One who gave His life for the life of the world, is the Watchman of the house. He is the Warder, faithful and true, of the temple courts of the Lord. –The Signs of the Times, February 12, 1902.

Christ knew just where to find John; and there, on the lonely island, He gave him a view of the closing scenes of this earth's history. . . . John was shown the slain Lamb of God, the Lion of the tribe of Judah, the Conqueror, standing in the midst of the seven golden candlesticks, which are the seven churches. –The Review and Herald, May 16, 1899.

**b. In the sermon given by Jesus on the mountain, what did He say about the light of the world?** Matthew 5:14–16.

Although there are evils existing in the church, and will be until the end of the world, the church in these last days is to be the light of the world that is polluted and demoralized by sin. –The Review and Herald, September 5, 1893.

No candlestick, no church, shines of itself. From Christ emanates all its light. –The Faith I Live By, p. 280.

As we walk in the commandments of God, we follow on in the way cast up for the ransomed of the Lord to walk in. The faithful of all ages have walked in this path, and they have shone as lights in the world. In this age the light transmitted from them has been shining with increased brightness upon the path of those who are walking in darkness. –The Review and Herald, April 25, 1893.

February 6

## 3. THE HOLY WATCHER

a. **What assurance does the Lord give that He always cares for His church?** Psalm 121:3, 4.

---

'Who walketh in the midst of the seven golden candlesticks' (Revelation 2:1). This scripture shows Christ's relation to the churches. He walks in the midst of His churches throughout the length and breadth of the earth. He watches them with intense interest to see whether they are in such a condition spiritually that they can advance His kingdom. Christ is present in every assembly of the church. He is acquainted with everyone connected with His service. He knows those whose hearts He can fill with the holy oil, that they may impart it to others. Those who faithfully carry forward the work of Christ in our world, representing in word and works the character of God, fulfilling the Lord's purpose for them, are in His sight very precious. –Testimonies, vol. 6, pp. 418, 419.

b. **To what is the true church of God compared, and how was it made up throughout the ages?** 1 Timothy 3:15.

The church is God's fortress, His city of refuge, which He holds in a revolted world. Any betrayal of the church is treachery to Him who has bought mankind with the blood of His only-begotten Son. From the beginning, faithful souls have constituted the church on earth. In every age the Lord has had His watchmen, who have borne a faithful testimony to the generation in which they lived. These sentinels gave the message of warning; and when they were called to lay off their armor, others took up the work. –The Acts of the Apostles, p. 11.

The church is the repository of the riches of the grace of Christ; and through the church will eventually be made manifest, even to 'the principalities and powers in heavenly places,' the final and full display of the love of God. . . . The church is God's fortress, His city of refuge, which He holds in a revolted world. . . . It is the theater of His grace, in which He delights to reveal His power to transform hearts. –Sons and Daughters of God, p. 13.

February 7

## 4. ONE CHURCH THROUGHOUT THE AGES

a. **What do we understand from the fact that the churches of seven cities in Asia Minor were selected by Christ to represent the Christian church?** Revelation 1:11.

---

"It was Christ who bade the apostle record that which was to be opened before him. 'What thou seest, write in a book,' He commanded, 'and send it unto the seven churches which are in Asia; unto Ephesus, and unto Smyrna, and unto Pergamos, and unto Thyatira, and unto Sardis, and unto Philadelphia, and unto Laodicea.' 'I am He that liveth, and was dead; and, behold, I am alive for evermore. . . . Write the things which thou hast seen, and the things which are, and the things which shall be hereafter; the mystery of the seven stars which thou sawest in My right hand, and the seven golden candlesticks' (Revelation 1:11, 18–20).

The names of the seven churches are symbolic of the church in different periods of the Christian Era. The number 7 indicates completeness, and is symbolic of the fact that the messages extend to the end of time, while the symbols used reveal the condition of the church at different periods in the history of the world. Christ is spoken of as walking in the midst of the golden candlesticks. Thus is symbolized His relation to the churches." –The Acts of the Apostles, pp. 585, 586.

"The Lord Jesus sent a mighty angel to make plain to John, by the use of symbols, the things that were to come to pass until the coming of Christ. He was bidden to write the instruction in a book for the benefit of the seven churches. This writing we now have preserved in the book of Revelation, but this book is understood by only a very few. It contains the message for the last days, and we are to dwell much upon these prophecies. –The Review and Herald, February 14, 1907.

b. **Why were only seven churches selected from the many others that existed in Asia? What does the number seven indicate?** Revelation 1:4.

---

"The Christ of Patmos had in His right hand seven stars. This assures us that no church faithful to their trust need fear of coming to naught; for not a star that has the protection of Omnipotence can be plucked from the hand of Christ. If a star separates itself from God, and falls from its setting, another will take its place. There will never be less than seven, this number being God's symbol of completeness. – Manuscript Releases, vol. 3, p. 359.

February 8

## 5. THE OBJECT OF SUPREME REGARD

a. **How does the Lord consider His people which are His church?** Deuteronomy 32:9, 10; Zechariah 2:8.

---

Through centuries of persecution, conflict, and darkness, God has sustained His church. Not one cloud has fallen upon it that He has not prepared for; not one opposing force has risen to counterwork His work, that He has not foreseen.–The Acts of the Apostles, pp. 11, 12.

To God, the dearest object on earth is His church. 'The Lord's portion is His people; Jacob is the lot of His inheritance. He found him in a desert land, and in the waste howling wilderness; He led him about, He instructed him, He kept him as the apple of His eye.'–The Signs of the Times, July 13, 1904.

b. **What will be the ultimate condition of God's remnant church?** Ephesians 5:25–27.

---

I saw that Christ will have a church without spot or wrinkle or any such thing to present to His Father, and as He leads us through the pearly gates of the New Jerusalem, or the golden city, Jesus will look upon His redeemed children and see of the travail of His soul and be satisfied.–Manuscript Releases, vol. 8, p. 225.

What does God's Word mean when it declares that Christ will present to Himself a church without spot or wrinkle or any such thing? It means that God's people can and must reach the standard of Christian perfection.–Ibid., vol. 14, p. 351.

February 9

**REVIEW AND THOUGHT QUESTIONS**

1. What qualities will the faithful steward possess?

_____

_____

2. What role does the church play in the closing work?

_____

_____

3. How has God's church been protected?

_____

_____

4. Which cities were chosen to represent the church?

_____

_____

5. What is the final condition of the remnant church?

_____

_____

# Ephesus

Desirable – (a.d. 27–100)

Lesson 7

Unto the angel of the church of Ephesus write (Revelation 2:1).

The True Witness bears testimony in commendation of the diligence of the church at Ephesus, declaring. 'I know thy works;' and all His commendations and reproofs are to be strictly regarded, for it is One who knows that speaks.–The Review and Herald, May 31, 1887.

*Suggested Readings*: The Acts of the Apostles, pp. 281–290. Maranatha, p. 15.

February 11

## 1. THE CITY OF EPHESUS

a. **What form of worship made Ephesus a religious center?** Acts 19:24–37.

In the days of the apostles, the city of Ephesus was famed for the worship of the goddess Diana and the practice of magic. The temple of Diana was considered, for its size and splendor, one of the wonders of the world. Its surpassing magnificence made it the pride of both the city and the nation.–The Signs of the Times, May 18, 1882.

b. **Who were the first converts at Ephesus, and how strongly were they defending the truth?** Acts 19:1–3; Revelation 2:2 (first part), 3.

On his arrival at Ephesus, Paul found twelve brethren, who, like Apollos, had been disciples of John the Baptist, and like him had gained some knowledge of the mission of Christ. They had not the ability of Apollos, but with the same sincerity and faith they were seeking to spread abroad the knowledge they had received.–The Acts of the Apostles, p. 282.

February 12

## 2. EVIL MEN AND FALSE APOSTLES

    **a. Although the condition of the church at Ephesus was desirable, what kind of men did they have to face?** Revelation 2:2 (last part); 1 Corinthians 15:32; 2 Corinthians 11:13.

The arrest [of Paul] was affected by the efforts of Alexander the coppersmith, who had so unsuccessfully opposed the apostle's work at Ephesus, and who now seized the opportunity to be revenged on one whom he could not defeat. Paul in his second Epistle to Timothy afterward referred to the machinations of this enemy of the faith: 'Alexander the coppersmith did me much evil. The Lord reward him according to his works.' In his first epistle he spoke in a similar manner of Hymeneus and Alexander as among those who 'concerning faith have made shipwreck;' 'whom,' he says, 'I have delivered unto Satan, that they may learn not to blaspheme.' These men had departed from the faith of the gospel, and furthermore had done despite to the Spirit of grace by attributing to the power of Satan the wonderful revelations made to Paul.–Sketches From the Life of Paul, p. 305.

    **b. Among the apostles there were some whom they found to be liars. Who were some of these liars?** Acts 5:1–10.

Not only to the early church, but to all future generations, this example of God's hatred of fraud and hypocrisy was designed to be a danger-signal. The brief but terrible history of Ananias and Sapphira has been traced for the benefit of all who profess to be followers of Christ. The punishment that overtook them should be a warning to all to guard against covetousness. It was covetousness that Ananias and Sapphira first cherished. The desire to retain for themselves a part of that which they had promised to the Lord led to fraud and hypocrisy.–The Review and Herald, February 2, 1911.

What is lying against the truth? It is claiming to believe the truth while the spirit, the words, the deportment, represent not Christ but Satan. To surmise evil, to be impatient and unforgiving, is lying against the truth; but love, patience, and long forbearance are in accordance with the principles of truth. Truth is ever pure, ever kind, breathing a heavenly fragrance unmingled with selfishness.–The SDA Bible Commentary [E. G. White Comments], vol. 7, p. 936.

February 13

## 3. A COMPLAINT AND A REPROOF

    a. **After the commendation of Jesus for the good work done by the church at Ephesus, what did Jesus remark?** Revelation 2:4.

The words of the True Witness should be carefully studied by all: 'I have somewhat against thee, because thou hast left thy first love'– grown cold, unsympathetic; hardness of heart has taken the place of brotherly, Christlike love.–The Review and Herald, February 9, 1892.

[Revelation 2:4 quoted.] Those mentioned in this scripture as losing their first love were not ranked with open sinners. They had the truth; they were established in the doctrine; they were firm to condemn and resist evil. Yet God declared, 'Nevertheless I have somewhat against thee.' They were losing their realization of the greatness of the love that God has shown for fallen humanity by making an infinite sacrifice to redeem them.–Ibid., February 25, 1904.

    b. **What was the cause of the early Christians losing their first love?** John 13:34, 35; 2 Timothy 4:1–4; 1 Corinthians 11:31.

But the early Christians began to look for defects in one another. Dwelling upon mistakes, giving place to unkind criticism, they lost sight of the Saviour and of the great love He had revealed for sinners. They became more strict in regard to outward ceremonies, more particular about the theory of the faith, more severe in their criticisms. In their zeal to condemn others they forgot their own errors. They forgot the lesson of brotherly love that Christ had taught. And, saddest of all, they were unconscious of their loss. They did not realize that happiness and joy were going out of their lives, and that soon they would walk in darkness, having shut the love of God out of their hearts.–Testimonies, vol. 8, p. 241.

But after a time the zeal of the believers began to wane, and their love for God and for one another grew less. Coldness crept into the church. Some forgot the wonderful manner in which they had received the truth. One by one the old standard-bearers fell at their post. . . . In their desire for something novel and startling [some of the younger workers] attempted to introduce new phases of doctrine, more pleasing to many minds, but not in harmony with the fundamental principles of the gospel.–The Act of the Apostles, p. 580.

February 14

## 4. WARNING BEFORE REJECTION

    a. **What warning and counsel was given to the church at Ephesus which is also extended to our time?** Revelation 2:5.

---

The message to the church at Ephesus is a close, decided personal testimony to them for leaving their first love, and an earnest call to repentance, lest their candlestick be moved out of its place. We need to heed these words of warning, and repent of our sins.–The Home Missionary, November 1, 1897.

The call to repentance is one that cannot be disregarded without peril. A belief in the theory of the truth is not enough. To present this theory to unbelievers does not constitute you a witness for Christ. The light that gladdened your heart when you first understood the message for this time, is an essential element in your experience and labors, and this has been lost out of your heart and life. Christ beholds your lack of zeal, and declares that you have fallen, and are in a perilous position.–Selected Messages, bk. 1, pp. 370, 371.

    b. **Under what condition is there hope for a church or an individual that is in danger of losing the first love?** 2 Chronicles 7:14; Jeremiah 18:8; Ezekiel 18:31.

---

The only hope for churches today is to repent and do their first work. The name of Jesus does not kindle the heart with love. A mechanical, formal orthodoxy has taken the place of deep, fervent charity and tenderness to one another. Will any give heed to the solemn admonition, 'Turn ye, turn ye; for why will ye die?' Fall upon the Rock, and be broken; then let the Lord Jesus prepare you, to mold and fashion you, as a vessel unto honor. Well may the people fear and tremble under these words: 'Except thou repent, I will come unto thee quickly, and will remove thy candlestick out of his place.' What then? 'If therefore the light that is in thee be darkness, how great is that darkness!'

The Spirit will not always strive with the heart that is filled with perversity. The infinite, forbearing One, who paid the price of His own blood to save His people, is addressing them. Who will hearken to His warning?"–Manuscript Releases, vol. 16, pp. 102, 103.

February 15

## 5. WONDERFUL PROMISES

a. **What other commendation is given to the church at Ephesus and why?** Revelation 2:6.

___

The death of God's beloved Son on the cross shows the immutability of the Law of God. His death magnifies the Law and makes it honorable, and gives evidence to man of its changeless character....

But the doctrine is now largely taught that the Gospel of Christ has made the Law of God of no effect; that by 'believing' we are released from the necessity of being doers of the word. But this is the doctrine of the Nicolaitans, which Christ so unsparingly condemned." –The Signs of the Times, February 25, 1897.

b. **What promise is given to the overcomer in this period?** Revelation 2:7.

___

The fruit of the tree of life in the Garden of Eden possessed supernatural virtue. To eat of it was to live forever. Its fruit was the antidote of death. Its leaves were for the sustaining of life and immortality. But through man's disobedience death entered the world. Adam ate of the tree of the knowledge of good and evil, the fruit of which he had been forbidden to touch. This was his test. He failed, and his transgression opened the floodgates of woe upon our world.–Medical Ministry, p. 233.

February 16

**REVIEW AND THOUGHT QUESTIONS**

1. Why does the word "Ephesus" represent the early church?

_____

_____

2. Who hindered the work of the early church?

_____

_____

3. What caused the downfall of this church period?

_____

_____

4. What hope was given to the early church?

_____

_____

5. What was promised to the overcomers at Ephesus?

_____

_____

# Smyrna

Sweet Perfume – (a.d. 100–323)

Lesson 8

And unto the angel of the church in Smyrna write; These things saith the first and the last, which was dead, and is alive (Revelation 2:8).

The forgiveness of sins is promised to him who repents, justification to him who believes, and the crown of life to him who is faithful unto death.– The SDA Bible Commentary [Ellen G. White Comments], vol. 7, p. 916.

**Suggested Readings**: The Acts of the Apostles, pp. 529–538. The Great Controversy, pp. 39–48.

February 18

## 1. JESUS CHRIST IS ALIVE

a. **Knowing the terrible persecution and martyrdom that would befall the Christians of the Smyrna period, what assurance did Jesus give them?** Revelation 1:18; 2:8.

Jesus read the future of His disciples. He saw one brought to the scaffold, one to the cross, one to exile among the lonely rocks of the sea, others to persecution and death. He encouraged them with the promise that in every trial He would be with them.–The Desire of Ages, p. 669.

b. **At the resurrection of Lazarus, what did Jesus say to Martha about Himself?** John 11:23–26.

Still seeking to give a true direction to her faith, Jesus declared, 'I am the resurrection, and the life.' In Christ is life, original, unborrowed, underived. 'He that hath the Son hath life' (1 John 5:12). The divinity of Christ is the believer's assurance of eternal life. 'He that believeth in Me,' said Jesus, 'though he were dead, yet shall he live: and whosoever liveth and believeth in Me shall never die. Believest thou this?' Christ here looks forward to the time of His second coming. Then the righteous dead shall be raised incorruptible, and the living righteous shall be translated to heaven without seeing death.–The Desire of Ages, p. 530.

February 19

## 2. POVERTY AND RICHES

    a. **What was always the material condition of God's people throughout the ages?** Revelation 2:9 (first part); Zephaniah 3:12.

The Lord's people are mainly made up of the poor of this world, the common people. Not many wise, not many mighty, not many noble are called. God 'hath chosen the poor of this world. The poor have the gospel preached to them.' The wealthy are called, in one sense; they are invited, but they do not accept the invitation.–Evangelism, p. 565.

The early Christians were indeed a peculiar people. Their blameless deportment and unswerving faith were a continual reproof that disturbed the sinner's peace. Though few in numbers, without wealth, position, or honorary titles, they were a terror to evildoers wherever their character and doctrines were known. Therefore they were hated by the wicked, even as Abel was hated by the ungodly Cain. For the same reason that Cain slew Abel, did those who sought to throw off the restraint of the Holy Spirit, put to death God's people.–The Great Controversy, p. 46.

    b. **What kind of wealth is recommended to us? 1 Timothy 6:17–19. What example did Jesus Himself give?** 2 Corinthians 8:9.

The humblest and poorest of the true disciples of Christ who are rich in good works, are more blessed and more precious in the sight of God than the men who boast of their great riches. They are more honorable in the courts of Heaven than the most exalted kings and nobles who are not rich toward God. The admonition which the apostle Paul exhorted Timothy to give the rich is applicable to very many who profess to believe the truth for these last days.–The Review and Herald, January 15, 1880.

Those who impart to others of the riches of the grace of heaven, will be themselves enriched. The ministering angels are waiting, longing, for channels through which they can communicate the treasures of heaven. Men and women can reach the highest stage of mental and moral development only by cooperating with Jesus in unselfish effort for the good of others. We are never so truly enriched as when we are trying to enrich others. We can not diminish our treasure by sharing it. The more we enlighten others, the brighter our light will shine.–Ibid., April 4, 1907.

February 20

## 3. THE SYNAGOGUE OF SATAN

a. **What does it mean to be a "Jew"?** John 8:39; Romans 2:28, 29.

---

The Pharisees had declared themselves the children of Abraham. Jesus told them that this claim could be established only by doing the works of Abraham. The true children of Abraham would live, as he did, a life of obedience to God. They would not try to kill One who was speaking the truth that was given Him from God. In plotting against Christ, the rabbis were not doing the works of Abraham. A mere lineal descent from Abraham was of no value.–The Desire of Ages, pp. 466, 467.

b. **What is the "synagogue of Satan"?** Revelation 2:9 (last part).

---

Christ speaks of the church over which Satan presides as the synagogue of Satan. Its members are the children of disobedience. They are those who choose to sin, who labor to make void the holy law of God. It is Satan's work to mingle evil with good, and to remove the distinction between good and evil. Christ would have a church that labors to separate the evil from the good.–The Review and Herald, December 4, 1900.

c. **What does the Bible say the synagogue of Satan will acknowledge, and when will this happen?** Revelation 3:9.

---

Soon we heard the voice of God like many waters, which gave us the day and hour of Jesus' coming. The living saints, 144,000 in number, knew and understood the voice, while the wicked thought it was thunder and an earthquake. When God spoke the time, He poured upon us the Holy Ghost, and our faces began to light up and shine with the glory of God, as Moses' did when he came down from Mount Sinai... At our happy, holy state the wicked were enraged, and would rush violently up to lay hands on us to thrust us into prison, when we would stretch forth the hand in the name of the Lord, and they would fall helpless to the ground. Then it was that the synagogue of Satan knew that God had loved us who could wash one another's feet and salute the brethren with a holy kiss, and they worshiped at our feet."–Early Writings, p. 15.

February 21

## 4. FAITHFUL UNTO DEATH

a. **Under what condition would the promise be fulfilled to those who endured the ten prophetic days of tribulation?** Revelation 2:10.

---

What an example have the martyrs for Jesus left us in their lives of self-denial and sacrifice. They were faithful and true to principle. Although prisons, tortures, inquisitions, gibbets, and the stake threatened them, they counted not their lives dear unto themselves. Their love for the truth was here manifested. They chose to obey the truth at the expense of great suffering. The world was not worthy of these heroes of faith. They died for their faith. The pure gold was refined from all dross through trial and suffering. As these shall enter the portals of glory they will shout in triumph: We overcame by the blood of the Lamb, and by the word of our testimony. We were faithful unto death, and now receive a crown of life.–The Review and Herald, December 2, 1875.

b. **To whom else is given the promise of receiving a crown of life, and when will it be given?** 2 Timothy 4:7, 8.

---

It was through one who declared himself to be a 'brother, and companion in tribulation' (Revelation 1:9), that Christ revealed to His church the things that they must suffer for His sake. Looking down through long centuries of darkness and superstition, the aged exile saw multitudes suffering martyrdom because of their love for the truth. But he saw also that He who sustained His early witnesses would not forsake His faithful followers during the centuries of persecution that they must pass through before the close of time.–The Acts of the Apostles, p. 588.

The cross of Calvary is a pledge to us of everlasting life. Faith in Christ means everything to the sincere believer. The merits of Jesus blot out transgressions, and clothe us with the robe of righteousness woven in the loom of heaven. The crown of life is presented before us as the honor to be given at the end of the conflict.–Evangelism, pp. 186, 187.

But we are to run the race, at the end of which is a crown of immortality and everlasting life. Yes, a far more exceeding and eternal weight of glory will be awarded to us as the prize when the race is run. 'We,' says the apostle, 'an incorruptible.'–Counsels on Health, p. 47.

February 22

## 5. ETERNAL DEATH

a. **What wonderful promise is given to the overcomer in the period of Smyrna?** Revelation 2:11.

'The wages of sin is death; but the gift of God is eternal life through Jesus Christ our Lord' (Romans 6:23). While life is the inheritance of the righteous, death is the portion of the wicked. Moses declared to Israel: 'I have set before thee this day life and good, and death and evil' (Deuteronomy 30:15). The death referred to in these scriptures is not that pronounced upon Adam, for all mankind suffer the penalty of his transgression. It is 'the second death' that is placed in contrast with everlasting life.–The Great Controversy, p. 544.

We shall receive either eternal life or eternal death. There is no middle ground, no second probation. We are called upon to overcome in this life as Christ overcame.–The SDA Bible Commentary [E. G. White Comments], vol. 6, p. 1112.

b. **What wonderful invitation is extended to everyone to escape from the second death?** Ezekiel 18:23, 31; Isaiah 55:7.

The word of God plainly tells us that few will be saved, and that the greater number of those, even, who are called will prove themselves unworthy of everlasting life. They will have no part in heaven, but will have their portion with Satan, and experience the second death.–Testimonies, vol. 2, pp. 293, 294.

Repentance is one of the first-fruits of saving grace. Repentance includes sorrow for sin, and a turning away from it.–The Signs of the Times, June 28, 1905.

February 23

**REVIEW AND THOUGHT QUESTIONS**

1. What did the future hold for Christ's church?

2. What is the true wealth of the Christian?

3. Who composes the synagogue of Satan?

4. To whom is the crown of life promised?

5. Who will suffer the second, eternal death?

# Pergamos

Elevation, Exaltation (a.d. 323–538)

Lesson 9

For the mystery of iniquity doth already work (2 Thessalonians 2:7).

What was the origin of the great apostasy? How did the church first depart from the simplicity of the gospel?–The Great Controversy, p. 384.

**Suggested Readings**: The Great Controversy, pp. 49-60. Maranatha, p. 161.

February 25

## 1. THE TWO-EDGED SWORD

a. **How did Jesus introduce Himself to the church at Pergamos?** Revelation 2:12.

b. **What should the Christian use, and what is it able to accomplish?** Ephesians 6:17; Hebrews 4:12.

Let the truth do the cutting; the word of God is as a sharp, two-edged sword and will cut its way to the heart. Those who know that they have the truth should not, by the use of harsh and severe expressions, give Satan one chance to misinterpret their spirit.–Testimonies, vol. 9, p. 239.

c. **What was the condition of the church during the period of Pergamos?** 2 Thessalonians 2:7.

Little by little, at first in stealth and silence, and then more openly as it increased in strength and gained control of the minds of men, 'the mystery of iniquity' carried forward its deceptive and blasphemous work. Almost imperceptibly the customs of heathenism found their way into the Christian church. The spirit of compromise and conformity was restrained for a time by the fierce persecutions which the church endured under paganism.–The Great Controversy, p. 49.

February 26

## 2. SATAN'S SEAT

a. What desire was developed by Lucifer? Isaiah 14:13, 14. What would be the ultimate result of such a desire? Proverbs 16:18; Isaiah 14:15.

---

Lucifer had said, 'I will be like the Most High' (Isaiah 14:12, 14); and the desire for self-exaltation had brought strife into the heavenly courts, and had banished a multitude of the hosts of God. Had Lucifer really desired to be like the Most High, he would never have deserted his appointed place in heaven; for the spirit of the Most High is manifested in unselfish ministry. Lucifer desired God's power, but not His character. He sought for himself the highest place, and every being who is actuated by his spirit will do the same. Thus alienation, discord, and strife will be inevitable. Dominion becomes the prize of the strongest. The kingdom of Satan is a kingdom of force; every individual regards every other as an obstacle in the way of his own advancement, or a steppingstone on which he himself may climb to a higher place.–The Desire of Ages, pp. 435, 436.

b. When tempting Jesus, what position did Satan claim as legitimately belonging to him? Luke 4:5, 6; John 12:31.

---

Satan, in his pride and arrogance, had declared himself to be the rightful and permanent ruler of the world, the possessor of all its riches and glory, claiming homage of all who lived in it, as though he had created the world and all things that were therein. . . . He endeavored to make a special contract with Christ, to make over to Him at once the whole of his claim, if He would worship him. . . .well concealed his true character and purposes that Christ did not recognize him as the fallen rebel chief whom He had conquered and expelled from heaven. . . . Satan knew that if Jesus should die to redeem man, his power must end after a season, and he would be destroyed. Therefore, it was his studied plan to prevent, if possible, the completion of the great work which had been commenced by the Son of God. If the plan of man's redemption should fail, he would retain the kingdom which he then claimed. And if he should succeed, he flattered himself that he would reign in opposition to the God of heaven."–Selected Messages, bk. 1, pp. 286, 287.

Satan had flattered himself in his first temptation that he had so

February 27

## 3. GOD'S FAITHFUL SERVANTS

a. How zealous were the early Christians in proclaiming the gospel? What was the fate of God's faithful servant "Antipas"? Revelation 2:13.

---

I was carried forward to the time when heathen idolaters cruelly persecuted and killed the Christians. Blood flowed in torrents. The noble, the learned, and the common people were alike slain without mercy. Wealthy families were reduced to poverty, because they would not yield their religion. Notwithstanding the persecution and sufferings which these Christians endured, they would not lower the standard. They kept their religion pure. I saw that Satan exulted and triumphed over their sufferings. But God looked upon His faithful martyrs with great approbation.–Early Writings, p. 210.

Looking upward by faith, [the early church Christians] saw Christ and angels leaning over the battlements of heaven, gazing upon them with the deepest interest and regarding their steadfastness with approval....

In vain were Satan's efforts to destroy the church of Christ by violence. The great controversy in which the disciples of Jesus yielded up their lives did not cease when these faithful standard-bearers fell at their post. By defeat they conquered. God's workmen were slain, but His work went steadily forward. The gospel continued to spread and the number of its adherents to increase."–The Great Controversy, p. 41.

b. What was foretold by the apostle Paul about those who will serve the Lord with a godly life? 2 Timothy 3:12. Why is it that persecution is not so strong today against Christians?

---

There is another and more important question that should engage the attention of the churches of today. The apostle Paul declares that 'all that will live godly in Christ Jesus shall suffer persecution' (2 Timothy 3:12). Why is it, then, that persecution seems in a great degree to slumber? The only reason is that the church has conformed to the world's standard and therefore awakens no opposition. The religion which is current in our day is not of the pure and holy character that marked the Christian faith in the days of Christ and His apostles. It is only because of the spirit of compromise with sin, because the great truths of the word of God are so indifferently regarded, because there is so little vital godliness in the church, that Christianity is apparently so popular with the world.–The Great Controversy, p. 48.

February 28

## 4. THE DOCTRINE OF BALAAM

a. What was Balaam's suggestion to Balac, King of Moab, about the children of Israel? Numbers 25:1-3; 31:16.

___

At first there was little intercourse between the Israelites and their heathen neighbors, but after a time Midianitish women began to steal into the camp. Their appearance excited no alarm, and so quietly were their plans conducted that the attention of Moses was not called to the matter. It was the object of these women, in their association with the Hebrews, to seduce them into transgression of the law of God, to draw their attention to heathen rites and customs, and lead them into idolatry. These motives were studiously concealed under the garb of friendship, so that they were not suspected, even by the guardians of the people.

At Balaam's suggestion, a grand festival in honor of their gods was appointed by the king of Moab, and it was secretly arranged that Balaam should induce the Israelites to attend. He was regarded by them as a prophet of God, and hence had little difficulty in accomplishing his purpose. Great numbers of the people joined him in witnessing the festivities. They ventured upon the forbidden ground, and were entangled in the snare of Satan. Beguiled with music and dancing, and allured by the beauty of heathen vestals, they cast off their fealty to Jehovah."–Patriarchs and Prophets, p. 454.

b. What sins began to creep into the Christian church in the period of Pergamos? Revelation 2:14, 15; 2 Corinthians 6:14, 15, 16 (first part); Ephesians 5:3.

___

Most of the Christians at last consented to lower their standard, and a union was formed between Christianity and paganism. Although the worshipers of idols professed to be converted, and united with the church, they still clung to their idolatry, only changing the objects of their worship to images of Jesus, and even of Mary and the saints. The foul leaven of idolatry, thus brought into the church, continued its baleful work. Unsound doctrines, superstitious rites, and idolatrous ceremonies were incorporated into her faith and worship.–The Review and Herald, March 24, 1891.

March 1

## 5. PROMISE TO THE OVERCOMER

a. What will be the inevitable result if we do not heed the warning of Jesus and repent? Revelation 2:16.

___

The truth is the truth. It is not to be wrapped up in beautiful adornings, that the outside appearance may be admired. The teacher is to make the truth clear and forcible to the understanding and to the conscience. The word is a two-edged sword, that cuts both ways. It does not tread as with soft, slippered feet.–The Review and Herald, April 20, 1897.

b. What wonderful promises were given the church at Pergamos and also to us if we overcome? Revelation 2:17; Isaiah 56:4, 5.

___

Upon what ground may we claim the full and rich promises of God? We can claim them only when we have fulfilled the conditions prescribed in His word. The Lord is constantly giving. He pours down the rain and the sunshine. He promises to give to His people the privilege of eating of the tree of life, and the hidden manna. He holds forth the crown of life, the white stone with the new name written therein.–The Review and Herald, December 17, 1889.

Immortal glory and eternal life is the reward that our Redeemer offers to those who will be obedient to Him. He has made it possible for them to perfect Christian character through His name and to overcome on their own account as He overcame in their behalf. He has given them an example in His own life, showing them how they may overcome.–Testimonies, vol. 3, p. 365.

March 2

REVIEW AND THOUGHT QUESTIONS

1. What position should the word of God have in our lives?

_____

_____

2. What does Satan claim as his own?

_____

_____

3. What will happen to those who oppose Satan's claim?

_____

_____

4. What did compromise bring to the church?

_____

_____

5. What is the promise to those who overcome worldly compromise?

_____

_____

# Thyatira

Sacrifice of Contrition (a.d. 538–1798)

Lesson 10

And unto the angel of the church in Thyatira write; These things saith the Son of God, who hath his eyes like unto a flame of fire, and his feet are like fine brass (Revelation 2:18).

The 1260 years of papal supremacy began in a.d. 538, and would therefore terminate in 1798.–The Great Controversy, p. 266.

**Suggested Readings**: The Great Controversy, pp. 61–78. Maranatha, p. 175.

March 4

1. **THE SON OF GOD**

   a. **How did Jesus identify Himself to the church of Thyatira?** Revelation 2:18.

   b. **What unmistakable evidence do we have that Jesus Christ is God, and is to be worshiped?** John 1:1–4, 14; Hebrews 1:5, 6.

   c. **In contrast, what was foretold in prophecy concerning the "son of perdition"?** 2 Thessalonians 2:3, 4.

The apostle Paul, in his second letter to the Thessalonians, foretold the great apostasy which would result in the establishment of the papal power. . . . Even at that early date he saw, creeping into the church, errors that would prepare the way for the development of the papacy.–The Great Controversy, p. 49.

The 'man of sin,' which is also styled the 'mystery of iniquity,' 'the son of perdition,' and 'that wicked,' represents the papacy, which, as foretold in prophecy, was to maintain its supremacy for 1260 years. This period ended in 1798.–Ibid., p. 356.

March 5

## 2. COMMENDATION AND REBUKE

a. **What positive characteristics of the church existed even under persecution?** Revelation 2:19.

Notwithstanding all the persecution of the saints, living witnesses for God's truth were raised up on every hand. Angels of the Lord were doing the work committed to their trust. They were searching in the darkest places and selecting out of the darkness men who were honest in heart.–Early Writings, p. 222.

b. **What false worship was introduced into the Christian church?** Revelation 2:20.

All false worship is spiritual adultery. The second precept, which forbids false worship, is also a command to worship God, and Him only serve. The Lord is a jealous God. He will not be trifled with. He has spoken concerning the manner in which He should be worshiped. He has a hatred of idolatry; for its influence is corrupting.–The SDA Bible Commentary [E. G. White Comments], vol. 1, p. 1106.

The man of sin was to arise, and do his work of exaltation and blasphemy, before the brethren could look for the coming of Christ. That great event was to be preceded by a falling away. There would be revealed a form of Antichrist, and the leaven of apostasy was to work with increasing power to the end of time.–The Review and Herald, July 31, 1888.

c. **What were the works of Jezebel?** 1 Kings 16:31; 18:4; 21:5–14.

I was carried back to the time of Ahab. God would have been with Ahab if he had walked in the counsel of heaven. But Ahab did not do this. He married a woman given to idolatry. Jezebel had more power over the king than God had. She led him into idolatry, and with him the people.–The SDA Bible Commentary [E. G. White Comments], vol. 2, p. 1033.

Jezebel then decided, as she could not make Elijah feel her murderous power, that she would be revenged by destroying the prophets of God in Israel. No one who professed to be a prophet of God should live.–The Review and Herald, September 23, 1873.

March 6

### 3. MOTHER AND DAUGHTERS

    a. **The "woman Jezebel" is represented in chapter 17 as Babylon the Great. Explain what made her drunk.** Revelation 17:3-6.

---

In the thirteenth century was established that most terrible of all the engines of the papacy–the Inquisition. The prince of darkness wrought with the leaders of the papal hierarchy. In their secret councils Satan and his angels controlled the minds of evil men, while unseen in the midst stood an angel of God, taking the fearful record of their iniquitous decrees and writing the history of deeds too horrible to appear to human eyes. 'Babylon the great' was 'drunken with the blood of the saints.' The mangled forms of millions of martyrs cried to God for vengeance upon that apostate power.–The Great Controversy, pp. 59, 60.

    b. **What are the characteristics of spiritual Jezebel, "Babylon the great," and who are her daughters?** Ezekiel 16:44.

---

Babylon is said to be 'the mother of harlots.' By her daughters must be symbolized churches that cling to her doctrines and traditions, and follow her example of sacrificing the truth and the approval of God, in order to form an unlawful alliance with the world. The message of Revelation 14, announcing the fall of Babylon must apply to religious bodies that were once pure and have become corrupt. Since this message follows the warning of the judgment, it must be given in the last days; therefore it cannot refer to the Roman Church alone, for that church has been in a fallen condition for many centuries. . . . 'Thou didst trust in thine own beauty, and playedst the harlot because of thy renown' (Ezekiel 16:14, 15).–The Great Controversy, pp. 382, 383. [Author's italics.]

In Revelation 17 Babylon is represented as a woman, a figure which is used in the Scriptures as the symbol of a church. A virtuous woman represents a pure church, a vile woman an apostate church. Babylon is said to be a harlot; and the prophet beheld her drunken with the blood of saints and martyrs. The Babylon thus described represents Rome, that apostate church which has so cruelly persecuted the followers of Christ. But Babylon the harlot is the mother of daughters who follow her example of corruption.–The Spirit of Prophecy, vol. 4, p. 233.

March 7

## 4. A TIME OF TRIBULATION

**a. What did Christ predict about that terrible time of persecution, and what hope was given to the believers?** Matthew 24:21, 22.

---

Amid the gloom that settled upon the earth during the long period of papal supremacy, the light of truth could not be wholly extinguished. In every age there were witnesses for God–men who cherished faith in Christ as the only mediator between God and man, who held the Bible as the only rule of life, and who hallowed the true Sabbath.–The Great Controversy, p. 61.

In the Saviour's conversation with His disciples upon Olivet, after describing the long period of trial for the church–the 1260 years of papal persecution, concerning which He had promised that the tribulation should be shortened–He thus mentioned certain events to precede His coming, and fixed the time when the first of these should be witnessed: 'In those days, after that tribulation, the sun shall be darkened, and the moon shall not give her light' (Mark 13:24). The 1260 days, or years, terminated in 1798. A quarter of a century earlier, persecution had almost wholly ceased.–Ibid., p. 306.

**b. What words of the apostle Paul were fulfilled by the faithful Waldenses?** 2 Timothy 2:19.

---

But of those who resisted the encroachments of the papal power, the Waldenses stood foremost. In the very land where popery had fixed its seat, there its falsehood and corruption were most steadfastly resisted. For centuries the churches of Piedmont maintained their independence; but the time came at last when Rome insisted upon their submission. After ineffectual struggles against her tyranny, the leaders of these churches reluctantly acknowledged the supremacy of the power to which the whole world seemed to pay homage. There were some, however, who refused to yield to the authority of pope or prelate. They were determined to maintain their allegiance to God and to preserve the purity and simplicity of their faith. A separation took place. Those who adhered to the ancient faith now withdrew; some, forsaking their native Alps, raised the banner of truth in foreign lands; others retreated to the secluded glens and rocky fastnesses of the mountains, and there preserved their freedom to worship God.–The Great Controversy, p. 64.

March 8

## 5. THE OVERCOMERS OF THYATIRA

   a. **Because of the fierce persecution during the period of Thyatira, what assurance was given to the faithful?** Revelation 2:24, 25.

While, under the pressure of long-continued persecution, some compromised their faith, little by little yielding its distinctive principles, others held fast the truth. Through ages of darkness and apostasy there were Waldenses who denied the supremacy of Rome, who rejected image worship as idolatry, and who kept the true Sabbath. Under the fiercest tempests of opposition they maintained their faith. Though gashed by the Savoyard spear, and scorched by the Romish fagot, they stood unflinchingly for God's word and His honor.–The Great Controversy, p. 65.

   b. **What wonderful promise was given to the church that remained faithful in the time of the dark ages?** Revelation 2:26–29.

Except among the Waldenses, the word of God had for ages been locked up in languages known only to the learned; but the time had come for the Scriptures to be translated and given to the people of different lands in their native tongue. The world had passed its midnight. The hours of darkness were wearing away, and in many lands appeared tokens of the coming dawn.

In the fourteenth century arose in England the 'morning star of the Reformation.' John Wycliffe was the herald of reform, not for England alone, but for all Christendom. The great protest against Rome which it was permitted him to utter was never to be silenced."–The Great Controversy, pp. 79, 80.

March 9

**REVIEW AND THOUGHT QUESTIONS**

1. Who has attempted to take the place of Christ?

_____

_____

2. What errors crept into the Thyatiran church?

_____

_____

3. Who are the daughters of Babylon?

_____

_____

4. What are the results of tribulation on the church?

_____

_____

5. What is promised to those who overcome tribulation?

_____

_____

# Sardis

That Which Remains [Remnant] (a.d. 1798–1833)

Lesson 11

And unto the angel of the church in Sardis write; These things saith he that hath the seven Spirits of God, and the seven stars; I know thy works, that thou hast a name that thou livest, and art dead (Revelation 3:1).

In the message to the church at Sardis two parties are presented–those who have a name to live, but are dead; and those who are striving to overcome. Study this message, found in the third chapter of Revelation.–The Review and Herald, August 20, 1903.

*Suggested Readings*: The Great Controversy, pp. 289–298. Maranatha, p. 238.

March 11

## 1. ALIVE BUT DEAD

a. **What words were spoken by Jesus to assure us of His tender care for His church?** Revelation 3:1 (middle part).

God's promise to His church will stand fast forever. He will make her an eternal excellence, a joy of many generations. There is no limit to His power. Our covenant-keeping Saviour unites with the omnipotence of the King of kings the tender care of a faithful shepherd. He who has chosen Christ has joined Himself to a power that no array of human wisdom or strength can overthrow.–The Review and Herald, October 8, 1903.

b. **What contrast exists between the profession of the church of Sardis and her real condition?** Revelation 3:1 (last part); James 2:17. **How is true faith demonstrated?**

Faith and works go hand in hand; they act harmoniously in the work of overcoming. Works without faith are dead, and faith without works is dead. Works will never save us; it is the merit of Christ that will avail in our behalf. Through faith in Him, Christ will make all our imperfect efforts acceptable to God.–Faith and Works, pp. 48, 49.

March 12

## 2. SEEKING FOR STRENGTH

a. **What counsel is given in the Word of God for those who are tempted to be discouraged?**
Revelation 3:2 (first part); Hebrews 12:12, 13.

---

There are times when under adversity and sorrow, the servants of God become discouraged and despondent. They brood over their circumstances, and, contrasting their condition with the prosperity of those who have no thought or care for eternal things, they feel aggrieved.–The Signs of the Times, February 3, 1888.

Often He met those who had drifted under Satan's control, and who had no power to break from his snare. To such a one, discouraged, sick, tempted, fallen, Jesus would speak words of tenderest pity, words that were needed and could be understood. Others He met who were fighting a hand-to-hand battle with the adversary of souls. These He encouraged to persevere, assuring them that they would win; for angels of God were on their side, and would give them the victory.

At the table of the publicans He sat as an honored guest, by His sympathy and social kindliness showing that He recognized the dignity of humanity; and men longed to become worthy of His confidence."–Gospel Workers, p. 47.

b. **What was the charge given against the church of Sardis regarding her works and why?**
Revelation 3:2 (last part).

---

Faith is made perfect by works. The cry will come to us from the servers of Mammon: You are too exacting; we cannot be saved by works. Was Christ exacting? He placed the salvation of man, not upon his believing, not upon his profession, but upon his faith made perfect by his works. Doing, and not saying merely, was required of the followers of Christ. Principle is always exacting. . . .

That religion which leads its subjects to enclose themselves in monastic walls, excluding themselves from their fellow men, and not doing the good they might, cannot be the light of the world. The world is no better for their living in it, because they shed no beams of light in good works. These live for themselves, and bring no glory to the Master, for they hide away from man as though ashamed of the light which they claim to have."–The Signs of the Times, January 15, 1880.

March 13

## 3. AS A THIEF IN THE NIGHT

a. **What would happen if those in Sardis would not repent and obey the truth they had heard?** Revelation 3:3 (first part).

---

'Hold fast.' This does not mean, Hold fast to your sins; but, Hold fast to the comfort, the faith, the hope, that God has given you in His Word. Never be discouraged. A discouraged man can do nothing. Satan is seeking to discourage you, telling you it is of no use to serve God, that it does not pay, and that it is just as well to have pleasure and enjoyment in this world.–The SDA Bible Commentary [E. G. White Comments], vol. 7, p. 959.

'Remember therefore how thou hast received and heard, and hold fast and repent. If therefore thou shalt not watch, I will come on thee as a thief, and thou shalt not know what hour I will come upon thee.' Here is the work which every son and daughter of God must do. But to adorn the doctrine of Christ our Saviour, we must have the mind that was in Christ. Our likes and dislikes, our desire to be first, to favor self to the disadvantage of others, must be overcome. The peace of God must rule in our hearts. Christ must be in us a living, working principle.–The Review and Herald, August 24, 1897.

Why repent? Because there have come in faults in the form of theories so subtle that by the influence of mind upon mind–through the agency of those who have departed from the faith–the wily foe will cause you imperceptibly to be imbued with the spirit that will draw you away from the faith.–Manuscript Releases, vol. 12, p. 126.

b. **What is the meaning of the words "I will come on thee as a thief"?** Revelation 3:3 (last part); 1 Thessalonians 5:2, 4.

---

Let every soul be on the alert. The adversary is on your track. Be vigilant, watching diligently lest some carefully concealed and masterly snare shall take you unawares. Let the careless and indifferent beware lest the day of the Lord come upon them as a thief in the night. Many will wander from the path of humility, and, casting aside the yoke of Christ, will walk in strange paths. Blinded and bewildered, they will leave the narrow path that leads to the city of God.

A man cannot be a happy Christian unless he is a watchful Christian. He who overcomes must watch; for, with worldly entanglements, error, and superstition, Satan strives to win Christ's followers from Him."–Testimonies, vol. 8, pp. 99, 100.

March 14

## 4. WHITE RAIMENT

a. What does the Lord promise to those who do not defile their garments? Revelation 3:4, 5 (first part); Zechariah 3:4, 5.

---

Every defect in character, every point in which they fail to meet the divine standard, is an open door by which Satan can enter to tempt and destroy them. . . .We are to exert every energy of the soul in the work of overcoming, and to look to Jesus for strength to do what we cannot do of ourselves. No sin can be tolerated in those who shall walk with Christ in white. The filthy garments are to be removed, and Christ's robe of righteousness is to be placed upon us. By repentance and faith we are enabled to render obedience to all the commandments of God, and are found without blame before Him. Those who shall meet the approval of God are now afflicting their souls, confessing their sins, and earnestly pleading for pardon through Jesus their Advocate. Their attention is fixed upon Him, their hopes, their faith, are centered on Him, and when the command is given, 'Take away the filthy garments, and clothe him with change of raiment, and set a fair miter upon his head,' they are prepared to give Him all the glory of their salvation.–Testimonies, vol. 5, p. 472.

b. **Why is it necessary to be clothed with white raiment, and what does it symbolize?** Matthew 22:11–14; Revelation 19:8.

---

We should consider the great sacrifice that was made in our behalf, to purchase for us the robe of righteousness, woven in the loom of heaven.–The Youth's Instructor, January 30, 1896.

Christ's white robe of righteousness will never cover any soul that is found in sin unrepented of and unforsaken. 'Sin is the transgression of the law.' Therefore those who are trampling upon the law of God, and teaching others to disregard its precepts, will not be clothed with the righteousness of Christ. Jesus came not to save people in their sins, but from their sins. 'And hereby we do know that we know him, if we keep his commandments. He that saith, I know him, and keepeth not his commandments, is a liar, and the truth is not in him.'–The Review and Herald, August 28, 1894.

March 15

## 5. CONFESSING CHRIST

a. **What did Jesus say should be a reason for great satisfaction and rejoicing, and why?** Luke 10:20; Revelation 20:15; 21:27.

The names of all those who have once given themselves to God are written in the book of life, and their characters are now passing in review before Him. Angels of God are weighing moral worth. They are watching the development of character in those now living, to see if their names can be retained in the book of life. A probation is granted us in which to wash our robes of character and make them white in the blood of the Lamb. Who is doing this work? Who is separating from himself sin and selfishness?–The SDA Bible Commentary [E. G. White Comments], vol. 7, p. 960.

b. **In what way may we confess Christ or deny Him, and what will be the ultimate result?** Revelation 3:5 (last part); Matthew 10:32, 33; Romans 10:9.

He who would confess Christ must have Christ abiding in him. He cannot communicate that which he has not received. The disciples might speak fluently on doctrines, they might repeat the words of Christ Himself; but unless they possessed Christlike meekness and love, they were not confessing Him. A spirit contrary to the spirit of Christ would deny Him, whatever the profession. Men may deny Christ by evilspeaking, by foolish talking, by words that are untruthful or unkind. They may deny Him by shunning life's burdens, by the pursuit of sinful pleasure.–The Desire of Ages, p. 357.

March 16

**REVIEW AND THOUGHT QUESTIONS**

1. How is true faith demonstrated?

2. How is faith made perfect by works?

3. Why is repentance an important work?

4. What is the white raiment?

5. How can we confess Christ?

# Philadelphia

Brotherly Love (a.d. 1833–1844)

Lesson 12

We know that we have passed from death unto life, because we love the brethren (1 John 3:14).

Christians are to cultivate self-restraint, love, forbearance, and unity one
to another by the cords of brotherly love.–The Review and Herald,
November 27, 1894.

*Suggested Readings*: The Great Controversy, pp. 317–330. Maranatha, p. 247.

March 18

### 1. THE KEYS OF DAVID

a. **What was foretold in prophecy concerning the keys of David?** Isaiah 22:20–22.

But clearer light came with the investigation of the sanctuary question. [The early adventist believers] now saw that they were correct in believing that the end of the 2300 days in 1844 marked an important crisis.–The Great Controversy, p. 429.

b. **As repeated by John in Revelation, when was the prophecy of Isaiah 22:22 fulfilled?** Revelation 3:7, 8.

Then I was shown that the commandments of God and the testimony of Jesus Christ relating to the shut door could not be separated, and that the time for the commandments of God to shine out with all their importance, and for God's people to be tried on the Sabbath truth, was when the door was opened in the most holy place in the heavenly sanctuary, where the ark is, in which are contained the ten commandments. This door was not opened until the mediation of Jesus was finished in the holy place of the sanctuary in 1844.–Early Writings, p. 42.

March 19

## 2. WORSHIPING AT THE SAINTS' FEET

a. **How is the synagogue of Satan described, and what do they say?** Revelation 3:9 (first part).

---

Satan has a large confederacy, his church. Christ calls them the synagogue of Satan because the members are the children of sin. The members of Satan's church have been constantly working to cast off the divine law, and confuse the distinction between good and evil. Satan is working with great power in and through the children of disobedience to exalt treason and apostasy as truth and loyalty.–Testimonies to Ministers, p. 16.

Satan has a church upon the earth which outnumbers the church of Christ. Christ calls it the 'synagogue of Satan,' because its members are the children of sin and transgression. They have ceased to honor God, they have cast His divine law aside, they have confounded the distinction between good and evil. But the world's Redeemer will have a church in which these essential differences will be made apparent, where the character of God will be represented.–The General Conference Bulletin, April 1, 1897.

b. **Who are the members of the synagogue of Satan and what will they do?** Revelation 3:9 (last part).

---

The 144,000 were all sealed and perfectly united. On their foreheads was written, God, New Jerusalem, and a glorious star containing Jesus' new name. At our happy, holy state the wicked were enraged, and would rush violently up to lay hands on us to thrust us into prison, when we would stretch forth the hand in the name of the Lord, and they would fall helpless to the ground. Then it was that the synagogue of Satan knew that God had loved us who could wash one another's feet and salute the brethren with a holy kiss, and they worshiped at our feet.–Early Writings, p. 15.

You think that those who worship before the saint's feet (Revelation 3:9) will at last be saved. Here I must differ with you; for God showed me that this class were professed Adventists, who had fallen away, and 'crucified to themselves the Son of God afresh, and put him to an open shame.' And in the 'hour of temptation,' which is yet to come, to show out everyone's true character, they will know that they are forever lost; and overwhelmed with anguish of spirit, they will bow at the saint's feet.–A Word to the Little Flock, p. 12.

March 20

## 3. THE HOUR OF TEMPTATION

a. **What encouraging promise is given to them that trust wholly in God?** 1 Corinthians 10:13.

God sometimes allows Satan to tempt His children, that they may be proved and tested. If they rely on their own strength, they will fail in the trial, but if they realize their inability to help themselves, and trust wholly in God, He will provide a way of escape. There are times when it is necessary for men to be exposed to danger, and to be placed among corrupting influences, but a sense of their dependence on God will lead them to keep their hearts uplifted to Him in prayer every hour, for strength to resist and grace to overcome. The experience gained in these fierce conflicts fortifies the soul to pass unscathed through more trying ordeals.–The Signs of the Times, March 29, 1905.

At times the masterly power of temptation seems to tax our will power to the uttermost, and to exercise faith seems utterly contrary to all the evidences of sense or emotion; but our will must be kept on God's side. We must believe that in Jesus Christ is everlasting strength and efficiency.–Our High Calling, p. 124.

b. **In order to be delivered from Satan's temptations, what should we do?** Revelation 3:10; James 4:7.

c. **Especially when will this experience be a reality?** Psalm 91:14, 15.

Do not think that you can safely drift with the current. If you do, you will surely become the helpless prey of Satan's devices. By diligent searching of the Scriptures and earnest prayer for divine help prepare the soul to resist temptation. The Lord will hear the sincere prayer of the contrite soul and will lift up a standard for you against the enemy. But you will be tried; your faith, your love, your patience, your constancy will be tested.–In Heavenly Places, p. 184.

The hour of temptation is to come upon all the world, to try them that dwell upon the earth; and although we do not wish to make a time of trouble for ourselves, nor do we wish to groan over trials in the future, still we should be so closely connected with God that we shall not fall under the temptation when it does come.–The Review and Herald, April 15, 1890.

March 21

## 4. STEADFAST TO THE END

   a. **What promise of Jesus should encourage us all along our Christian race?** Revelation 3:11 (first part); 22:12.

---

'This same Jesus which is taken up from you into heaven, shall so come in like manner as ye have seen him go into heaven.' Precious, indeed, was this promise to those sorrowing disciples, that they should again see Jesus who was greatly beloved by them all. Precious also is this promise to every true follower of Christ. None who truly love Jesus will be sorry that He is coming again. And as they approach nearer to the coming of the Son of man, the true lovers of Jesus will look forward with joyous hope, and will seek to get all ready to behold Him whom their souls loveth, who died to redeem them.–The Youth's Instructor, April 1, 1854.

We are pilgrims and strangers on the earth. Our sojourn here is as it were the Christian's winter. But our faith and hope reach forward and upward to the better life, to the home that Christ has gone to prepare for those that love Him. . . .

There are many things to be overcome. Day by day the battle goes on. The struggle is lifelong; for Satan watches every opportunity to take advantage of us, that he may ensnare us to our ruin."–Manuscript Releases, vol. 18, p. 138.

   b. **To whom will the crown of life be given and when?** Revelation 3:11 (last part); Matthew 24:13; 2 Timothy 4:7, 8.

---

'Behold, I come quickly: hold that fast which thou hast, that no man take thy crown.' Here again we are admonished to faithfulness, in view of the conflict. We must not yield any point that we have already gained. . . . We are seeking for a crown, a crown of glory that fadeth not away. As overcomers we are to reign with Christ in the heavenly courts; and we are to overcome through the blood of the Lamb and the word of our testimony.–The Review and Herald, July 9, 1908.

If it were possible for us to be admitted into heaven as we are, how many of us would be able to look upon God? How many of us have on the wedding-garment? How many of us are without spot or wrinkle or any such thing? How many of us are worthy to receive the crown of life?–Maranatha, p. 98.

March 22

## 5. THE REMNANT OF PHILADELPHIA

a. **What promise is given to the overcomers of Philadelphia, and who are they?** Revelation 3:12, 13.

While I was praying at the family altar, the Holy Ghost fell upon me, and I seemed to be rising higher and higher, far above the dark world. I turned to look for the Advent people in the world, but could not find them, when a voice said to me, 'Look again, and look a little higher.' At this I raised my eyes, and saw a straight and narrow path, cast up high above the world. On this path the Advent people were traveling to the city, which was at the farther end of the path.... Soon we heard the voice of God like many waters, which gave us the day and hour of Jesus' coming. The living saints, 144,000 in number, knew and understood the voice, while the wicked thought it was thunder and an earthquake.–Early Writings, pp. 14, 15.

b. **Following the example of the Philadelphian church, what should we cultivate if we want to be overcomers?** John 13:34, 35.

God wants us to love one another. He says, 'By this shall all men know that ye are my disciples, if ye have love one to another,' 'as I have loved you; that ye also love one another.' This is the new commandment. It was new because Christ had not, before it was spoken, given the evidence of how much He loves us.–The General Conference Bulletin, April 3, 1901.

[The disciples] were to love one another as Christ had loved them. These were their credentials that Christ was formed within, the hope of glory.–The SDA Bible Commentary [E. G. White Comments], vol. 5, p. 1141.

March 23

**REVIEW AND THOUGHT QUESTIONS**

1. What event would close the Philadelphian period?

2. Who constitutes the synagogue of Satan?

3. How are we to deal with temptation?

4. Who will receive the crown of life?

5. What is the promise given to Philadelphia?

# Laodicea

Judgement of the People (a.d. 1844–the End)

Lesson 13

As many as I love, I rebuke and chasten: be zealous therefore, and repent (Revelation 3:19).

The message to the Laodicean church is applicable to all who have had great light and many opportunities, and yet have not appreciated them. –The Faith I Live By, p. 306.

**Suggested Readings**: The Acts of the Apostles, pp. 593–602. The Great Controversy, pp. 662–678.

March 25

1. JESUS SPEAKS TO THE CHURCH

a. How does Jesus address the angel of the Laodicean church? Revelation 3:14.

Some will not receive the testimony that God has given us to bear, flattering themselves that we may be deceived and that they may be right. They think that the people of God are not in need of plain dealing and of reproof, but that God is with them. These tempted ones, whose souls have ever been at war with the faithful reproving of sin, would cry: Speak unto us smooth things. What disposition will these make of the message of the True Witness to the Laodiceans? There can be no deception here. This message must be borne to a lukewarm church by God's servants.–Testimonies, vol. 3, p. 259.

b. What startling message does Jesus give about the condition of the angel of the church? Why is this condition unacceptable? Revelation 3:15, 16.

Halfhearted Christians are worse than infidels; for their deceptive words and noncommittal position lead many astray. The infidel shows his colors. The lukewarm Christian deceives both parties. He is neither a good worldling nor a good Christian. Satan uses him to do a work that no one else can do.–The SDA Bible Commentary [E. G. White Comments], vol. 7, p. 963.

March 26

## 2. DIAMETRICALLY OPPOSED

    a. **What do the angel and the people of the Laodicean church think and state of their own condition, and what is Christ's answer?** Revelation 3:17.

---

[Revelation 3:14–17 quoted.] The Lord here shows us that the message to be borne to His people by ministers whom He has called to warn the people is not a peace-and-safety message. It is not merely theoretical, but practical in every particular. . . .

What greater deception can come upon human minds than a confidence that they are right when they are all wrong! The message of the True Witness finds the people of God in a sad deception, yet honest in that deception. They know not that their condition is deplorable in the sight of God. While those addressed are flattering themselves that they are in an exalted spiritual condition, the message of the True Witness breaks their security by the startling denunciation of their true condition of spiritual blindness, poverty, and wretchedness. The testimony, so cutting and severe, cannot be a mistake, for it is the True Witness who speaks, and His testimony must be correct."–Testimonies, vol. 3, pp. 252, 253.

    b. **Why is it that the condition of "thou knowest not" is the most dangerous?** John 9:40, 41.

---

The Pharisees were spiritually blind, and were leaders of the blind. The physical blindness that Jesus had healed in the man born blind, was not as dangerous as the moral blindness of those who had evidence piled upon evidence in regard to the divine character of the world's Redeemer, and yet who closed the eyes of their understanding, and refused to see, because they were too self-exalted to be instructed by Christ. They claimed to be learned in the Scriptures, to have spiritual eyesight, yet they made the plainest specifications concerning Christ a different matter from that which the records testified. 'The land of Zabulon, and the land of Nephthalim, by way of the sea, beyond Jordan, Galilee of the gentiles; the people which sat in darkness saw great light; and to them which sat in the region and shadow of death light is sprung up.' The light of the world was shining amid the moral darkness, and the darkness comprehended it not.–The Signs of the Times, November 6, 1893.

March 27

## 3. A GENEROUS OFFER

   a. **Before a complete rejection takes place, what wonderful goods does Jesus offer to Laodicea?** Revelation 3:18.

---

As I have of late looked around to find the humble followers of the meek and lowly Jesus, my mind has been much exercised. Many who profess to be looking for the speedy coming of Christ are becoming conformed to this world and seek more earnestly the applause of those around them than the approbation of God. They are cold and formal, like the nominal churches from which they but a short time since separated. The words addressed to the Laodicean church describe their present condition perfectly. They are 'neither cold nor hot,' but 'lukewarm.' And unless they heed the counsel of the 'faithful and true Witness,' and zealously repent and obtain 'gold tried in the fire,' 'white raiment,' and 'eyesalve,' He will spew them out of His mouth.–Early Writings, pp. 107, 108. [Author's italics.]

The deadly lethargy of the world is paralyzing your senses. Sin no longer appears repulsive because you are blinded by Satan. The judgments of God are soon to be poured out upon the earth. 'Escape for thy life' is the warning from the angels of God. Other voices are heard saying: 'Do not become excited; there is no cause for special alarm.' Those who are at ease in Zion cry 'Peace and safety,' while heaven declares that swift destruction is about to come upon the transgressor.–Testimonies, vol. 5, p. 233.

   b. **What heavenly virtues are represented by the "gold," the "white raiment," and the "eyesalve"?** 1 Peter 1:7; Revelation 19:8.

---

Again and again has the voice from heaven addressed you. Will you obey this voice? Will you heed the counsel of the True Witness to seek the gold tried in the fire, the white raiment, and the eyesalve? The gold is faith and love, the white raiment is the righteousness of Christ, the eyesalve is that spiritual discernment which will enable you to see the wiles of Satan and shun them, to detect sin and abhor it, to see truth and obey it.

The deadly lethargy of the world is paralyzing your senses. Sin no longer appears repulsive because you are blinded by Satan."–Testimonies, vol. 5, p. 233.

March 28

## 4. BE ZEALOUS AND REPENT

a. **Since the destiny of the church hangs on the acceptance of the counsel of the true witness, what strong appeal does Jesus make to the angel?** Revelation 3:19.

---

I saw that the testimony of the True Witness has not been half heeded. The solemn testimony upon which the destiny of the church hangs has been lightly esteemed, if not entirely disregarded. This testimony must work deep repentance; all who truly receive it will obey it and be purified.–Early Writings, p. 270.

The displeasure and judgments of God are against those who persist in walking in their own ways, loving self, loving the praise of men. They will certainly be swept into the satanic delusions of these last days, because they received not the love of the truth. Because the Lord has, in former days, blessed and honored them, they flatter themselves that they are chosen and true, and do not need warning and instruction and reproof. The True Witness says, 'As many as I love, I rebuke and chasten: be zealous therefore, and repent.' The professed people of God have the charge against them, 'Nevertheless I have somewhat against thee, because thou hast left thy first love. Remember therefore from whence thou art fallen, and repent, and do the first works; or else I will come unto thee quickly, and will remove thy candlestick out of his place, except thou repent.'–The Review and Herald, December 23, 1890.

b. **What is the proof of a true and genuine repentance?** Ezekiel 33:14–16; Luke 19:8, 9.

---

There is no evidence of genuine repentance unless it works reformation. If he restore the pledge, give again that he had robbed, confess his sins, and love God and his fellow men, the sinner may be sure that he has found peace with God. Such were the effects that in former years followed seasons of religious awakening.–The Great Controversy, pp. 462, 463.

There are many who fail to understand the true nature of repentance. Multitudes sorrow that they have sinned and even make an outward reformation because they fear that their wrongdoing will bring suffering upon themselves. . . . Balaam, terrified by the angel standing in his pathway with drawn sword, acknowledged his guilt lest he should lose his life; but there was no genuine repentance for sin, no conversion of purpose, no abhorrence of evil.–Steps to Christ, p. 23.

March 29

## 5. STANDING AT THE DOOR AND KNOCKING

    a. **Since there was no evidence of repentance of the angel, to whom is Jesus now addressing His words?** Revelation 3:20. How does Christ knock at the door?

---

Christ waits at the door of the heart, saying, Open to Me; but He will not force Himself upon any one. Are we listening for His voice? Is our pride humbled and subdued by His divine compassion and pitying love? Open the door of the heart; for Christ is waiting to enter.–The Signs of the Times, February 3, 1898.

Says the true Witness, 'Behold, I stand at the door and knock.' Every warning, reproof, and entreaty in the word of God, or through his delegated messengers, is a knock at the door of the heart; it is the voice of Jesus, asking for entrance. With every knock unheeded, your determination to open becomes weaker and weaker. If the voice of Jesus is not heeded at once, it becomes confused in the mind with a multitude of other voices, the world's care and business engross the attention, and conviction dies away. The heart becomes less impressible, and lapses into a perilous unconsciousness of the shortness of time, and of the great eternity beyond.–The Review and Herald, November 2, 1886.

    b. **What special blessing is pronounced upon the overcomer in the period of Laodicea?** Revelation 3:21, 22.

---

'To him that overcometh will I grant to sit with Me in My throne, even as I also overcame, and am set down with My Father in His throne.' We can overcome. Yes; fully, entirely. Jesus died to make a way of escape for us, that we might overcome every evil temper, every sin, every temptation, and sit down at last with Him.–Testimonies, vol. 1, p. 144.

March 30

**REVIEW AND THOUGHT QUESTIONS**

1. What work does the lukewarm Christian do?
_____
_____

2. What is the true state of Laodicea?
_____
_____

3. How can we obtain the gold, white raiment and eyesalve?
_____
_____

4. How only can the true believer overcome?
_____
_____

5. What is granted to the Laodicean overcomer?
_____
_____

## OTHER BIBLE STUDY BOOKS

All audio books available on Amazon

Languages: English and Spanish

1. Bible study Guide: Fundamentals of the Bible Volume 1

2. Bible study Guide: Revelation Volume 2

## COMING SOON

1. Bible Study Guide: Stewardship

2. Bible Study Guide: Revelation Volume 3, 4 and 5.

3. Bible Study Guide: Daniel

4. Bible study Guide: Fundamentals of the Bible Volume 2, 3.

www.ingramcontent.com/pod-product-compliance
Lightning Source LLC
Chambersburg PA
CBHW060426010526
44118CB00017B/2381